RED SHADOWS

The aim of Zenith Books is to present the history of minority groups in the United States and their participation in the growth and development of the country. Through histories and biographies written by leading historians in collaboration with established writers for young people, Zenith Books will increase awareness of and at the same time develop an understanding and appreciation for minority group heritage.

ZENITH BOOKS SERIES CONSULTANT

John Hope Franklin
Professor of History, Howard University

ZENITH BOOKS ADVISORY BOARD

John Gearon
High School Social Studies Consultant, Chicago Public Schools

Rayford W. Logan
Professor of History, Howard University

Gordon McAndrew
Superintendent of Schools, Gary, Indiana

Joseph E. Penn
Supervising Director, Department of History, Public Schools of the District of Columbia

J. Rupert Picott
Assistant Director of Higher Education, National Education Association

Isadore Pivnick
Co-ordinator, Federal-State Projects, San Francisco Unified School District

Samuel Shepard, Jr.
Assistant Superintendent, St. Louis Public Schools

Hugh H. Smythe
Professor, Brooklyn College

C. S. Whitaker, Jr.
Chairman, Department of Afro-American Studies, Princeton University

Dr. John Hope Franklin, Chairman of the History Department at the University of Chicago, has also taught at Brooklyn College, Fisk University, and Howard University. For the year 1962–63, he was William Pitt Professor of American History and Institutions at Cambridge University in England. He is the author of many books, including *From Slavery to Freedom*, *The Militant South*, *Reconstruction After the Civil War*, and *The Emancipation Proclamation*.

Dan Georgakas was born in Detroit, Michigan. He attended Wayne State University, where he received a B.A. degree in history, and the University of Michigan, where he received his M.A. degree. In 1963, Mr. Georgakas was a member of a Fulbright Study group in Greece. His poetry has appeared in the following anthologies: *Where Is Vietnam*, *31 New American Poets*, *The Now Generation*, *Campfires of the Resistance*, *Thunderbolts of Peace and Freedom*, and many more. Currently, Mr. Georgakas is working on a book on the recent history of the city of Detroit and also a novel.

Another outstanding Zenith Book

The Broken Hoop, by Dan Georgakas. The history of native Americans from 1600 to 1890, from the Atlantic Coast to the Plains.

RED SHADOWS

The history of Native Americans
from 1600 to 1900, from
the desert to the Pacific Coast

DAN GEORGAKAS

ZENITH BOOKS
DOUBLEDAY & COMPANY, INC., GARDEN CITY, NEW YORK
1973

The Zenith Books edition, published simultaneously in hardbound and paperback volumes, is the first publication of *Red Shadows*.

Zenith Books Edition: 1973
ISBN: 0-385-06889-1 Trade
          0-385-06916-2 Paperbound
Library of Congress Catalog Card Number 74–175375

COVER CREDIT: Navajo blanket with twelve figures from Navajo, New Mexico, courtesy of Museum of the American Indian, Heye Foundation, New York, New York.

CONTENTS

INTRODUCTION   9

PART I—GREAT PAINTED LADY: THE SOUTHWEST
    Land of the Sun   15
    The Rain Lovers   17
    The Peaceful People   22
    The Great Learners   27
    The Raiders   37

PART II—WHERE THE SUN FALLS INTO THE SEA:
    CALIFORNIA
    Death in the Missions   57
    Captain Jack   63
    Ishi, Last of the Yahi   73

PART III—NO MORE FOREVER: THE NORTHWEST
    Potlatchers and Totem Poles   87
    The Longest March   101

INDEX   123

INTRODUCTION

When Columbus discovered America in 1492, he called it the New World. Five hundred years before Columbus, roving Vikings had discovered America and called it Vineland. Thousands of years before the Vikings, Phoenicians and possibly Egyptians may have discovered America when blown off course by storms. But at least ten thousand years before any of these explorers, the ancestors of the Indians had been the first people to discover America. They became the Native Americans.

Most scholars believe the Native Americans' ancestors crossed from Siberia to Alaska by means of what was then either a land bridge or short waterway between Asia and North America. One skull found in California indicates that these people may have been living in North America as early as 20,000 B.C. At another place what appears to be a man-made fireplace dates back to 30,000 B.C.

By the time of Columbus, the Native Americans had developed over two thousand languages and major dialects, more than in all of Europe and Asia. Rather than alphabets, Indians used picture symbols to help their remarkable memories retain their rich oral tradition of songs, stories, poetry, and rituals. Their eloquence has become renowned. Wherever possible in the pages that follow, direct quotes and Indian poetic imagery will be utilized. The earth will be Great Painted Lady. Citizens of the

United States will be people of the eagle. Concepts such as *forever* will be put in the Indian form as *long as the grass shall grow and the water flow.*

The Native Americans greeted the first Europeans with friendship and hospitality. Their legends told of a tribe of lost white brothers who would some day be reunited with them. The Indians were hurt and then angered when the white people did not act as brothers. The white tribes wanted to destroy Indian religion and to make Indians work as slaves. They wanted to take away minerals and to possess land. The Native Americans believed there was great harmony in the universe, but they could not understand how the white people fit into that harmony. The advance of the Europeans seemed to destroy the order of the ages. First the eastern woodlands, the swamps, and the plains, then the desert, the coast, and the mountains of the West were overrun and parceled out by the whites. The buffalo were slaughtered and the salmon depleted. Disease and war killed off the majority of Indians. The others were forced on reservations where their traditions were systematically destroyed. The last survivor of one of the California tribes put it simply, "You stay, I go." But as Chief Seattle of the Spokane prophesied, the spirits of the departed linger. By the banks of lonely rivers and in the wilderness of steel canyons, red shadows whisper there are other ways of living than we now live and other ways of dreaming than we now dream.

Banks of the Musconetcong
Delaware Country
1973

Part I

Young Apache girl wearing her finest traditional clothing and jewelry. (*Huntington Free Library, Heye Foundation*)

Great Painted Lady:
THE SOUTHWEST

*If the Great Father wants my braves
to cease attacks across the Texas
border, he will have to remove
Texas far enough away so my young
men cannot find it.*

Satanta (Kiowa)

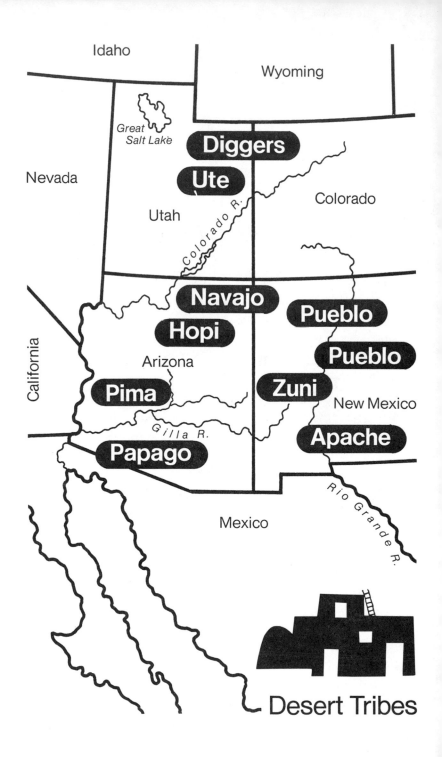

Idaho

Wyoming

Great Salt Lake

Nevada

Diggers

Ute

Utah

Colorado R.

Colorado

Navajo

Navajo

California

Arizona

Hopi

Pueblo

Pueblo

Pima

Zuni

New Mexico

Gilla R.

Papago

Apache

Rio Grande R.

Mexico

Desert Tribes

LAND OF THE SUN

Vast plateaus seem to roll forever under the all powerful sun. In the distance, mountains peak to elegant heights and almost touch the clear blue that carries magnificent thunderhead clouds that only too rarely release the rains that never quite satisfy the endless thirst of the parched earth. The white dunes sometimes take a blood red color or become painted deserts. It is a vast and quiet region, but to the Indians who made it their home, there was no such thing as emptiness. Everything was alive with spirit power. Even the heavens above were filled with the wandering souls of the dead and numberless supernatural beings. Only in some remote spot or in some sheltered silence of the night could the voices of these spirits be heard. Only by tireless contemplation could the totality and unity of all life be understood.

Where mountains intruded into the heat, the Indians knew they might find forests of aspen and the rich soil made by ancient lava flows. Caves inside such mountains might contain bats and ice, yet outside the sun was supreme. Occasionally lightning storms might crack the sky with white stitches of thunder and lightning, but the southwest desert, the area that became New Mexico and Arizona, primarily meant endless miles of wind-eroded, thirsting soil. Canyons cut by creeping rivers that were older than mankind made sudden plunges thousands of feet deep, the canyon walls a geological record of the time between the present and the ages before the dinosaurs. It was here the Grand Canyon had been carved, and it was here the colors were so spectacular the Indians called the earth Great Painted Lady.

Unlike the Indians of the eastern woodlands who created large political units such as the Iroquois League of the Five Nations, the people of the Southwest tended to live in small groups. In the southern part of Arizona around the Gila River there were cities of the Pima or River People. Directly to the south of them in the deserts were the Papago or Desert People. In New Mexico, the most important tribes were the Pueblo, who took their name from the style of homes they built. Some of the most famous of their cities were Zuñi, Taos, and the seven villages of the Hopi. To the east of the Pueblo where the deserts begin to give way to prairies, there were raiding tribes such as the Kiowa and Comanche who lived in the manner of the Plains people. To the west along the Colorado River, which is now one of the borders of California, there were the fierce Yuma and Mohave. But in New Mexico and Arizona, people were not much interested in war. The Hopi's name for themselves was Hopitu, the peaceful people. Warriors rarely bothered to hunt the scarce game of the arid region and the few weapons were mainly used for self-defense and occasional fights to show individual bravery.

The Southwesterners were essentially farming people. They had developed their agriculture to such a degree that they never had to worry about having enough food and thus had much leisure time for the dancing and singing they loved so much. Sometime around the year A.D. 1000 new tribes called Apache and Navajo entered the area. These newcomers from the North possessed a more advanced type of bow, and they wore skins and leather moccasins. They were much less organized than the farmers and rarely had permanent homes. They lived in deep canyons with good hiding places from which to base attacks on their prosperous neighbors. The raiders were often identified by their secondary or subtribal names, which usually came from the area they lived in. Among such names for the Apache were Mescalero Apache, Chiricahua Apache, and White Mountain Apache. A group of Apache even became officially adopted by the Kiowa and became known as Kiowa Apache. The raiders were not united by any government but felt a certain relationship because of similar languages and customs.

THE RAIN LOVERS

By the time Columbus touched America, the Pima and the Papago had been living in the same places for over three thousand years. They had built complicated irrigation canals to store water for their crops. Hunting and war were minimized, and men devoted their main energies to agriculture. Special varieties of maize or corn were developed with ceremonial significance attached to each type. These decentralized farmers were peaceful people. Survival was so dependent upon the rain that every ceremony and ritual, even those having to do with war, was tied to the need for rain. The Pima and Papago did not enjoy being warriors. Rather than speaking of personal bravery, a Papago warrior chanted how he had seized the enemy's "seeds and beautiful clouds and beautiful winds." All this disagreeable violence was for the purpose of guaranteeing the corn crop.

An important war song ends not with glorification of the killer but with a hymn to corn:

> *Then came forth a thick stalk and a thick tassel*
> *and the undying seed ripened.*
> *This I did to serve the people.*
> *This should you also think and desire,*
> *all you who are my kinsmen.*

The supernatural world of the Pima was ruled by Elder Brother, who had created people out of clay. Ceremonies often consisted of the retelling and acting out of his splendid deeds. The Pima also were in awe of animal spirits, which could communicate with both men and women, giving them special powers. The animal spirits had the important task of giving dreams. The rain lovers developed many rituals for these spirits and for Elder Brother. They often made an offering of prayer sticks. Among some groups the prayer sticks were made of eagle-feather down, which represented rain-bringing clouds. These prayer sticks were often decorated with sacred charms and symbols of wealth to indicate the giver's appreciation of the gift of rain. The sticks were sometimes left upon ceremonial grounds or important springs to indicate in what place the rain was desired. During rituals, basket drums were played in the belief that they were calling the clouds to council. One of the Pima songs which accompanied this music has the following passage:

> *hi-ya naiho-o! Pluck out the soft down*
> *from the breast of the eagle and turn it*
> *toward the west where small clouds sail*
> *hi-ya naiho-o! beneath the home*
> *of the rain gods it is thundering;*
> *large corn is there. hi-ya naiho-o!*

beneath the home of the rain gods
it is raining; small corn is there.

One of the most fertile areas of the corn growers was the
irrigated Gila Valley of Arizona, where the crop was in-
sured by an intricate and rational use of water. The villagers of the Gila had a drinking festival in which they
filled themselves with a beerlike alcohol just as the land was
supposed to fill itself with water. Their shamans or medicine men had authority only because of dream power and
because they were thought to be born with crystals within
their bodies that helped them heal. Women were sometimes thought to have crystals but were usually restricted
to healing children or helping at the time of birth. Shamans might lose their crystals or have them taken away if
they did something incorrectly. Shamans knew good songs
to help in a cure, and there were special healing singers for
diseases caused by animals. Often disease was thought to
come from doing a ritual incorrectly or having broken a
taboo. These psychological treatments were accompanied
by an impressive knowledge of curative herbs and potions.
Ultimately, the Pima and Papago were very practical about
medicine. If a shaman had a poor history of curing, he was
suspected of being an evil magician or a fake and could be
clubbed to death.

The clouds brought rain and the rain brought up the
corn. People dreamed of the wonderful spirits in the skies,
of all the marvels of their Great Painted Lady. Their poetry
expressed complex emotions through simple sentences and
sounds. Each word was designed to set off a chain reaction
of connected thoughts in the listening imagination. Con-
trasts and repetitions allowed the individual to reflect on
the many subtleties involved in a single word. Songs were
creative acts between humans and not entertainment by a

few for many. The curing song was part of the cure, just as the rain song was part of the actual cause of rain. Nothing disturbed them so much as to discover that the corn grew just as well for the songless whites. Nor could they understand how whites admired Indian songs without believing in their spiritual content. Creative expression and life were a unity. No other way was safe for the soul or the flesh.

The first known white people to intrude upon the rain lovers were the Spanish. Coronado touched Pima villages in 1540 during his futile search for the legendary Seven Cities of Gold. The decisive personality, however, was Father Kino, a Jesuit missionary who made evangelical tours in 1687. He baptized Pima by the hundreds and gave them Christian names. His work was made easier by the legends which told of a lost tribe of white brothers who were destined to return and help their Indian relatives. The black robe certainly had good magic. He had water rituals, magical names, a new crop called wheat, and fine new cattle. The Papago on the desert heard about the crusader and were eager to find out more about the teachings of the black robes. They began to make a yearly holiday out of going to Mexico to refresh their Christian water names and get beads and other magic charms. A hundred years passed without much change in Indian life. Mexico won independence from Spain in 1823, but the Pima and Papago barely noticed. Not even the coming of settlers from the United States created any difficulty. The newcomers were few in number and were uninterested in the places where the Indians lived. Only the defeat of Mexico by the United States in 1848 caused the first ripples of change. Now, the Pima and most of the Papago were under the direct rule of the United States. A few Pima became scouts for the United States during the war and continued afterwards in new wars against Indians, especially the Apache.

The pony soldiers liked the Pima but were annoyed at the long purification rites required when a warrior happened to kill a foe.

The Pima never made war on the United States and they were proud to boast they did not know the color of a white man's blood. Their territory continued to be outside the major arenas of white interest and ambition. They were farmers who did not object to quiet reservation life in the way the fierce Navajo and Apache did. There would have been little difficulty in bringing such peaceful, productive, and co-operative folk into an interdependent but equal relationship with the white system. But the greed of the whites would not permit it. Everything must be done as they wanted it done. Land must belong to individuals, not groups. Land must be bought and sold like a basket. Since the Pima did not resist, it was a simple matter to draw water from their rivers until the Indian canals went dry. No abrupt or startling event marked the end of Pima prosperity, but as the year 1900 approached, the Pima farms had to be abandoned. The Pima learned English. They adopted the white man's clothing, the white man's housing, and the white man's religion, yet the whites continued to regard them as inferiors. The once proud and wealthy Pima were reduced to poverty.

The Papago fared no better. After the Spanish came, they added wheat crops to their fields of corn. They bred herds of horses and cattle. They fought against the Apache. These changes in the old ways were minimal, but the coming to power of the United States was another matter. That meant reservations, and reservations meant moving to poor land and becoming impoverished. Rather than being prosperous farmers of their own lands, the Papago had to work in cotton fields for daily wages. Traditional clan relationships broke down into desperate individual struggles to survive. Physical comforts built up over centuries diminished. The unity and sympathy of tribal life became an unraveled cord. Like the Pima they withdrew into apathy as they grew poorer while watching the whites grow richer. Like the Pima, they drank too much. Like the Pima, they withdrew into a world of daydreams and memories. Like the Pima, they became listless. Their suffering was less dramatic but no less intense than that of the regal warrior societies of the plains. The world of the buffalo hunters had ended with a bang, the world of the rain lovers with a sigh.

THE PEACEFUL PEOPLE

The Pueblo lived north of the corn growers and took their name from the cliff dwellings of terraced apartments in which they lived. Villages containing hundreds of dwellings lined great streams or were built high on ragged cliffs like Acoma, the sky city. The Pueblo grew many kinds of crops but most important was corn. Their myth of creation spoke of a Sky Father who spread his hand palm downward over the earth and in every wrinkle of his skin there was a shining grain of yellow corn: "In the dark of the early world-dawn, they gleamed like sparks of fire."

Like their neighbors, the Pueblo were concerned with how to bring rain. Their prayers were not spontaneous expressions of an agitated soul but carefully memorized requests for a good life free of violence and drought. Rather than speak of their own personal affairs, the Pueblo sang of the movements of the sun, the problems of the different seasons, and the need that there be enough rain. Their beautiful songs and pageants did not celebrate the individual but the community. Anyone who thought of personal power was considered evil or insane.

The most beloved supernaturals were called the kachinas, two hundred happy cloud and rain beings. Special kachina societies impersonated these spirits by wearing masked costumes and frequently appearing in the plazas or at special events. The Pueblo felt they had a special relationship to these beings. If they fulfilled all their obligations, the rain would fall. The small kachina dolls now admired by tourists represent the full-scale costumes but have no sacred value. Originally, such dolls were used to teach the young about the special characteristics of individual kachinas.

People rest from their chores for a moment on one of the terraces of the Laguna Pueblo in 1879. (*National Archives*)

The Pueblo clowns were almost as popular as the kachinas. These beings who were dressed in amusing costumes were thought to be so mighty that they could say any blasphemy or obscenity they desired. They specialized in custard-pie-in-the-face type humor and jokes about love-making. Very often they were used by the community as a friendly method of criticizing a citizen for vanity or some other shortcoming.

The kachinas, clowns, and other ceremonial figures were controlled by priestly groups organized by strict regulations. Different sets of medicine men controlled different ceremonies and diseases under rights similar to modern patents, licenses, and copyrights. There was little room for the democratic and often egotistical spirit of the plains which sought direct communication with the spirits. The Pueblo man and woman found their worth in a group effort that meshed with what seemed to be a cosmic order. The pageantry of Pueblo ceremonies was a rare art form involving a whole community in laughter, reverence, and happiness. The appearance of the rain gods during one ceremony at the San Juan pueblo has been described thusly:

> Suddenly a deafening noise breaks loose from behind the blanket screen; the closely packed, dimly lit room stirs with joyful anticipation. There is a wild roar from the top of the room where the gods seem to have dropped suddenly, bringing with them frightening thunder, lovely bird songs & cricket chirps & the rhythmic jingling of a hundred tiny bells attached to their writhing waists and swiftly moving feet. The shrill hoots, the resounding whooping & the weird piercing sound which identify each individual rain god intermingle.

Life among the Pueblo was filled with such stirring events. Food was ample and shelter was comfortable, making Pueblo life among the most pleasant in all the Americas. The lack of hunting and war deaths meant males were not maimed or given to short lives. Courtship was minimal and divorce easy. Romance was not much talked about, but it was part of the ordinary life of the married and unmarried, with the same set of rules for women and men. Women had a certain power in that a man came to live in her house when they married. The husband usually kept his ceremonial property and other valuables at his mother's in case of trouble. Should the marriage work out, a man did not become an authoritarian father to his children but a friend and adviser, a role he also took with his sister's children.

Competition and violence were discouraged among the Pueblo. People even wore similar clothing to avoid jealousy. Life was bound to communal needs of the clan. At the time of marriage, clans, not individuals, gave gifts, and in case of marital problems, the clan advised. This vast and close-knit society based on blood ties and marriage vows made the Pueblo individual feel lost and naked when he had to act as a solitary striver in the white man's system of brutal competition.

The Pueblo had little fear of death. They believed the dead ones became clouds and would return with rain. Even so, the Pueblo felt a terrible loss when a loved one died. Members of the family might mourn for four seasons, sitting away from the common fire and rarely finding the energy to speak. The forceful, dominating, and explosive personality valued by the Europeans was unwelcome here. Pueblo society was based on many small cells, each having a mutual respect for all the differing parts. All were equally important and honored just as the ant and the mountain were equally honored in their religion. Hopi sand paintings were started on the outer edges and completed at the center. This gift of encircling and concentrating characterized Pueblo life. Their poetry was religious and their religion was poetic. They did not recite words but sang feelings. Sound was a power in and of itself. The method of the Pueblo was different from that of Europeans but the ultimate goal of happiness was much the same. One ceremony ended with a sacred figure saying,

> *Everything is open*
> *now go home*
> *& leave your worries*
> *& your tears*
> *& sadness.*

And the people responded,

> *Yes, oh yes, yes, yes.*

The mystic Pueblo had a legend of a tribe of lost brothers and they were overjoyed when the Spanish rode into their lives in 1540. This joy soon soured as the Spanish treated them brutally and tried to turn each Pueblo city into a conquered domain. The Pueblo learned about new fruit, vegetables, and tools, but the Spanish would not allow them horses. The Spanish imposed taxes which could be paid in labor time, crops, or finished products such as cloth. Catholicism was forced upon them, and the beloved masked dances forbidden. The Pueblo reasoned these were not the lost white brothers after all but some other tribe. Their gentle nature recoiled at Spanish cruelty, and in the great rebellion of 1680, they rose up and drove all the Spanish from their lands. The victory was short-lived, as the Spanish came back with more soldiers, and in ten years of ruthless combat they re-established their power.

The Spanish were heartless in their manner of ruling,

even cutting off arms and legs to prevent revolt. Many of the Pueblo went to live with the Navajo for safety, but eventually they realized the Spanish were going to remain. Some allowed the newcomers to protect them from raiders such as the Apache, and a few accepted Christianity. The passage of power from Spain to Mexico meant little to the Pueblo, but in 1848 when the United States seized the territory from Mexico, there was a new crisis. Other conquering powers had always recognized Pueblo civilization. The new rulers did not. They considered the Pueblo to be an inferior, stupid, and worthless race.

The Pueblo found themselves forced to take smaller and smaller reservations. The Navajo, their sometime allies, sometime enemies, became more numerous and more powerful until the Pueblo reservations were only pebbles in Navajo ponds. In spite of all hardships and setbacks, the Pueblo's religiously centered government survived. The Pueblo believe they know the secret of the universe. They are convinced a supreme world order of peace such as that long promised to them will be achieved. They resist any attempt to tamper with their ancient beliefs. They do not seek worldly power as most nations do. Power has never been their way. The Pueblo prefer to wait. Like oriental mystics, they feel much can be accomplished by doing nothing. Their patience is not a thing of minutes or days or even the two hundred years of the United States.

THE GREAT LEARNERS

The Apache and Navajo probably came from the northern lake tribes of Canada or Alaska if not from the Asian continent itself. The marauders were ignorant and possessed few material things. They lived by raiding and attempted to learn some of the skills of the Pueblo. The Navajo like most Indian tribes called themselves *the people* (*Dene*) but a more appropriate name for them might be the Great Learners for in a short period of time they would profoundly adapt their way of life twice, first under the influence of other Indians, then under the influence of the whites.

The Pueblo Revolt of 1680 cleared the Southwest of Spaniards as the usually peaceful village folk rose up against their conquerors. The Navajo had little to do with the actual rebellion, but when the Spanish renewed their conquests many of the Pueblo groups sought sanctuary with them. These Pueblo favorably and decisively altered the Navajo way of life. The Pueblo refugees often took Navajo mates, and the Pueblo partner always was the teacher. Agriculture underwent dramatic improvement. Houses changed. The quality of life was refined in a hundred subtle ways with the introduction of sheep flocks marking a basic change from the dependence on raiding. New clans came into existence. Even the Navajo physical type changed as plump figures with small hands and feet like the Pueblo became as common as the tall rangy builds that had previously characterized the tribe. The Navajo took the Pueblo mythology and rituals and added imaginative elements of their own. They were less concerned with rain as they had been hunters and fighters who did not even know the comforts of permanent settlements. They developed special songs and rituals to guarantee the health and luck of their hunters. Previously medicine men had visions which took them to spirit villages where they learned powerful songs and other magic. Now the medicine men adopted elaborate chants for their specific supplications. By 1770 this contact began to break off as the Pueblo returned to their old homes, but the Navajo bands in the nearby canyons were now bursting with new energy and consciousness. Their fighting men were ready for conquests. Their first period of learning was done. Raiding, weaving, agriculture, and trading had made them wealthy and now their herds of sheep and horses would give them a glorious afternoon in the southwest sun.

The Navajo had never had much contact with the Zuñi or Hopi Pueblos and thus felt free to plunder them at will. They raided with an intensity that expressed their determination never to experience poverty again. The most pathetic victims of Navajo warfare were the Diggers, who lived to the north in the area of the Salt Lake Basin. These people were probably the most miserable Indians in North America. They received their name from the fact that they dug roots from the desert floor in order to survive. They were so close to starvation most of the time that they developed almost no poetry, ritual, or social organization. The Diggers could offer no military resistance to the other tribes who took them to sell as slaves. Winter left them so weak and helpless, they actually had to be fattened up in order to survive the trip to places such as Santa Fe where trading for slaves went on. The Diggers were only victims in the slave trade but the Navajo, Apache, Comanche, Ute, Kiowa, and Mexicans were both raiders and raided upon.

Slavery in the West differed greatly from slavery on the plantations of the South. Among the Navajo, female slaves were usually given menial jobs or forced to tend sheep so that Navajo women could do the more intricate task of weaving. Many female slaves became wives, and children who were captured were often adopted as a member of the family. Adult males were not treated nearly so well. Slaves, especially women, were also traded for horses and sheep, which were an important base of wealth. The Navajo fought fiercely to get their share and to defend what they had, but their lives were not centered on war or slavery. One of their night chants has all the calmness of the peaceful Pueblo:

> *In beauty I walk*
> *With beauty before me I walk*
> *With beauty behind me I walk*
> *With beauty above me I walk*
> *With beauty above and about me I walk*
> *It is finished in beauty.*
> *It is finished in beauty.*

The Navajo who were taken as slaves by other Indians were treated pretty much as Navajo treated their own captives. Mexican owners were a bit different. They were more likely to treat female captives as mistresses rather than wives, and they were not very quick to adopt slave children as their own. Male slaves usually became fieldworkers although a lucky few picked up valuable skills which they taught to their own people if they were fortunate enough to escape. The willingness to learn something new, whether it was a skill in working precious metals such as gold or just learning to operate a new machine, was a characteristic of the Navajo. The only thing the Great Learners remained absolutely closed to was the Catholic Church. They simply would not convert.

Few Navajo had had any contact with the United States before 1846 when Kearny's Army of the West entered their lands as part of the Mexican War. These Missouri volunteers were not the usual type of soldier. They elected their own officers, and when Kearny asked them to march in dress uniform, they voted a resolution informing him that they had come to fight, not parade. This army wanted to make allies of the Navajo. The Indians were impressed with them as the soldiers gave good gifts, promised important privileges, and treated them as equals. At one meeting the Navajo and soldiers were even able to feast and dance together. The sounds of tom-toms, clapping hands, rattles, and whistling mingled before the campfire in a strange moment of friendship. Even so, the citizens of the parliamentary republic had no sense of the nature of the democracy they were encountering, a democracy in which no man could ever dictate to any other. Some of the Navajo resented the Americans as late-comers in the long struggle against the Mexicans, but as always, they were willing to acquire valuable allies, especially if they could be protected from other tribes. The Missourians voted to proceed to the interior of Navajo country where they spoke with all the important bands and made a favorable impression. Unfortunately there were too few soldiers to defend the Navajo and the democratic spirit of Kearny's men did not accurately reflect the policies of the United States. Other tribes continued to harass the Navajo. Mexicans continued to raid. The new allies themselves began to issue orders, often contradictory, often shifting from moon to moon. Before long, the Navajo decided to treat the bluecoats as they would any other powerful people. They would fight when cornered, raid when convenient, and flee when outnumbered. The United States soon understood that soldiers would have to be permanently stationed in Navajo country. In a spot the Indians called Green-Place-in-the-Rocks, the bluecoats built a stronghold named Fort Defiance.

The new fort made raiding more difficult but did not alter basic patterns. A few bands made peace, but ten years after the fort was built most Navajo still felt free to attack not only settlers but the fort itself. These bands were delighted when they heard the bluecoats had deserted Fort

Kit Carson, the army scout, destroyed Navajo herds and placed the people on reservations in 1863. (*Courtesy of Museum of the American Indian, Heye Foundation*)

Defiance. It was the first year of the Civil War and the soldiers were being recalled to fight against other whites, but the Navajo thought their own raids had finally exhausted the pony soldiers and driven them back to the lands they had come from. Emboldened by their "victory," the Navajo raided as never before. Sometimes approached by parties of soldiers in blue and sometimes by soldiers wearing a new gray uniform, the Navajo fought for their own ends in their own ways. They imagined the Southwest was to be their domain forever, but like so many nations at the height of their military might, the confident

Navajo did not know they were enjoying their last summer of power.

The Navajo upsurge was so devastating, the whites decided they must be dealt with at once in spite of the Civil War. Kit Carson, the famous scout, was appointed to subdue the Navajo. Colonel Carson never had more than seven hundred men under his command and he had to face a nation of over ten thousand. His campaign in 1863 lasted less than twelve months, and although he never killed more than fifty Navajo, he was completely successful in destroying the nation. The Indians had been brought up with one idea of terror and brutality, the whites with another. Carson gave twenty-dollar bounties for every horse or mule either captured or killed and one-dollar bounties for sheep. All the enemies of the Navajo enthusiastically took part in the slaughter. Carson himself methodically destroyed all the crops he could find. In one canyon where Navajo sometimes hid, he spent several days making certain that three thousand peach trees were destroyed. At another place he captured seventy-five thousand pounds of wheat. At still another spot, the land itself was burned to prevent reseeding. Carson made total war in a manner the Indians had never imagined. The hungry and shocked Navajo began to surrender by the hundreds and then by the thousands.

In a sad trek of three hundred miles which the Navajo have called the Long Walk, they were forced to move to a barren spot in New Mexico called the *Bosque Redondo*. A new fort was constructed in the area to police the bands and prevent escapes. The brutalities and deaths of the forced march to the distant sickly place were as horrible and as needless as the suffering the Cherokee had experienced in 1838 on their Trail of Tears, when they had been forced at gunpoint to move from the Carolinas to Oklahoma. The Navajo were sheepless, seedless, and hopeless. They languished for five heartbreaking years, learning nothing and barely surviving. Their pleas to have a reservation in their old territories were not met until they took a sacred oath that they would never raid again. It was a pledge they made and kept. Manuelito, an important Navajo chief, remembered the day the Navajo returned to their homeland. "We told the drivers to whip the mules, we were in such a hurry. When we saw the top of the mountain from Albuquerque we wondered if it was our mountain and we felt like talking to the ground we loved it so, and some of the old men and women cried with joy . . ."

The Navajo received some seeds for their new reservation land, and by 1869 some of them began to work with silver, a craft which would one day help lift some of them to relative financial security. But life was an unending trial during the first bitter years of reservation existence. There was continual trouble about cattle. Many tribesmen lived a few miles off the actual reservation and this created difficulties with the whites, although the reservations were eventually expanded to take in the already de facto Navajo land. Treacherous agents tricked them systematically. Traders exploited them as a matter of routine. The Indian Bureau methodically attempted to destroy every traditional custom. Fifteen years passed before the tools and wagons promised to them were delivered. The weather was terrible and the crops failed. There were never-ending delays in getting needed lands and tools. Many individuals lapsed into alcoholism, and the nation might have been overcome by the despondency that crippled so many tribes but for the women. Navajo women had always had an important place in tribal life. They had owned the sheep and had always had an equal voice in business matters. Now these resourceful and confident women put their en-

The work of silversmiths helped the Navajo to make a transition from their traditional way of life to life on the reservation. (*Courtesy of Museum of the American Indian, Heye Foundation*)

ergy into the art of weaving. Their rugs and blankets were done with such extraordinary skill that their fame quickly spread beyond the Southwest throughout the nation and even beyond both oceans.

In the slowest most painful sort of way, the earnings from silverwork and weaving allowed the tribe to grow. Sheep were bought and agricultural techniques mastered. The Navajo were the Great Learners and, at last, they found a way to live within the white man's framework. As the tribes around them grew poorer, the Navajo prospered. Once the Pueblo had dominated the region and the Navajo had been marauding outsiders. By mid-twentieth century the Navajo had become the largest and wealthiest tribe in the United States. But even in the midst of their success, there were Navajo who starved because there were many bands who fell into the pattern of the Pima and Papago. Their silverwork was not for their own pleasure and use but was a commodity to be sold as their weaving and admission to their sacred ceremonies were sold. Once there had been a time when the Navajo were poor, but they had all been poor together. Once there had been a time when the Navajo were rich, and they had all been rich together. Under the new system there were Navajo who held a million United States dollars and there were Navajo who died of malnutrition and starvation.

The traditional Navajo religion taught that the sun and the moon were bright shields carried by immortal beings on horseback. Such ideas were eventually mingled with Christian teachings but Navajo sand paintings remained as they had always been: the artist sits in the open or in a small hut and makes patterns with sand to guarantee the harmony of the universe. The colored sand is so skillfully sifted that true lines can be drawn as easily as circles and intricate configurations. The red, yellow, and black earth colors generally follow the pattern of a pair of lines in the center crossing at right angles upon which stand tall humanlike figures wearing masks. Many colored lines blend into the pattern to form reptiles, rainbows, and other natural elements. The paintings vary greatly in form and content, but their precision speaks of their importance. As the sand painter works, the Navajo live again. The history and the wisdom of the Navajo once more are released into the cosmos. The artist expresses his proud respect for all the natural phenomena, and when his design is done, he must smudge it out, for all life is temporary. Each hand makes a subtle variation in the most ancient design, but however full of joy and sorrow and struggle and beauty the design of any one day may be, it, too, will surely pass away just as in the new year, another hand will create yet another variation.

THE RAIDERS

Perhaps no tribe has been so maligned as the Apache. Partially this has to do with the nature of the tribe and partially because the Apache were among the last Indians to threaten the security of the United States. They came to the Southwest at the same time as the Navajo but unlike them, the Apache preferred to remain raiders and were never greatly influenced by Pueblo or Spanish ways. The Apache fought for property, not glory. They counted no coups and celebrated no scalp-taking. Those, who fought them rarely even saw them, for the Apache were the masters of camouflage and swift movement, able to vanish into the barren desert or mountains, to move faster on foot than pursuing cavalry on horses. They wore no feather headdresses for dime novelists to write glowing paragraphs about, and they valued the horse more for its food value than for beauty or transportation.

If there was little about the Apache to romanticize, they were still far from the heartless savages their enemies often made them out to be. The Apache roamed in small bands and one of the primary attributes of a leader was that he must not lose many warriors. A cousin of Geronimo has left a valuable record of that warrior's raiding and he states that life was held in such high regard that a victory dance would frequently be omitted if one of the band had been killed. Likewise the most important religious, aesthetic, and social event of the Apache had nothing to do with war or the military arts but concerned females at puberty. At this time the girl became White Painted Lady (mother earth) and complicated ceremonies retold the creation myths and took the girl through all the stages of her future life. Individuals who assisted a family at this ritual became as close to one another as mortal can be to mortal. Even in the midst of marauding and eluding U.S. cavalry, Geronimo's band always allowed for the puberty rituals.

Such regard for women and for the life of their fellow tribesmen was among the finest traits of the Apache. They thought peace in the heart was the principal virtue. Should a woman be captured on a raid, a man was not to have her unless he first opened her heart and won her through love. The Apache had hundreds of songs for this and similar purposes. Apache girls have written that people would fall in love by the campfires just by listening to songs. These melodies were often short and direct yet all the more charming and sensitive for their naïve frankness,

My sweetheart, we surely could have gone home.
But you were afraid!
When it was night, we surely could have gone home.
But you were afraid!

The Apache generally took no adult male prisoners unless they were to be sold as slaves, but children, especially boys, were often treated as natural offspring. They were taught that the highest virtues were to speak the truth, to pay their debts, and never to steal from their own kind. Only then could an individual know peace of heart. Clan and marital loyalties were primary, making Apache camps places of wit and good cheer. The bands loved all social activities, gambling, and sports. Their fondness for drink became legendary and was a large part of social life both on the reservations and off. They were constantly on the move and had no time to produce objects of beauty, yet like all peoples the Apache character had many levels. The killer raider of the trail was the joking lover of the campsite. He was also the one who taught children how to capture delicate butterflies and then release them without harm.

The bands liked to establish mountain strongholds from which to attack the neighboring pueblos and Mexican land. Apache women planted gardens of corn, beans, and squash, as well as harvesting cactus fruit. Their main staple was a meal made of corn and mesquite beans which had the double advantage of being easy to grow and light to carry. The principal source of wealth, however, was stolen property. Though the Apache disliked routine work and restraint of any kind, they had the patience to plan and execute complex ambushes. The Apache military strategy outwitted some of the best generals of West Point and many plans were co-ordinated over large areas even though the tribe operated in widely scattered units that were extremely jealous of their individual rights and independence.

The history of any given Apache group is almost impossible to trace because of certain taboos and because of the lack of written records. One of these taboos was that if an individual died, his name must not be repeated. The deeds of great warriors were thus quickly forgotten, but even more damage was done to the work of future historians if the man's name coincided with that of a common bird or animal, which was often the case. If the name of the dead man were Bald Eagle, the band would have to devise a new way of saying *bald* and *eagle*. The language was thus constantly changing. The grandmother in a family might not always be able to communicate with her grandchildren. Another taboo was that Apache must never eat creatures that lived in water. Likewise, although they hunted for the feathers of certain birds, many of the same birds were taboo as far as eating was concerned. Apache fear of the dead cannot be too much exaggerated. They liked to bury the deceased in daylight, if possible on the very day of death, and then immediately to cleanse themselves for fear of contamination. Their fear of the dead led to a terror of owls, whose voices were the song of death. A hooting owl in the night could frighten them as no human sound ever could.

While the various name taboos and fears of the dead have blotted much of Apache history, like most Indians the Apache had excellent memories. Many historians have noted that the memories of old people among the Sioux and Apache are more accurate than the written accounts of whites. Jason Betzinez, the cousin of Geronimo, broke many of the Apache taboos in his writing. As a teen-ager Betzinez fought with bow and arrow in a Stone Age struggle against the cavalry yet he lived to hear the blast of the atom and watch the flaming tails of guided missiles in the very same desert. This intriguing figure wrote of the Indian oral tradition,

> To the Indian it is a curious thing that white people accept as fact only that which is written on paper, whereas events retold by word of mouth, even if of greater importance, are disparaged as being mere folklore.

The relationship between the Apache and the Mexicans was so bitter that the Apache tended to trust the United States more than most Indians did. Nevertheless when the bluecoats arrived in force to put the Apache on reservations, the various bands resisted. The details of the army-Apache struggles are the familiar ones except for one unique episode. That exception concerns Cochise, one of the most able of the Chiricahua chiefs, and Tom Jeffords, a white adventurer. Cochise was a handsome man but like all Apache, when he painted his face to lead a group of shouting, excited, armed raiders, he looked fierce. Cochise explained Apache ways with these words:

> God made us not as you; we were born like the animals, in the dry grass, not on beds like you. This is why we do as the animals, go about at night and rob and steal. If had such things as you have, I would not do as I do, for then I would not need to do so.

Apache fury, however, was not the cause of Cochise going to war with the whites. He had always been at peace with the United States until 1860 when a young officer tricked him into bringing his family to dine at an army camp. A boy had recently been stolen by some Indians and the officer intended to hold Cochise and his family as hostages. Cochise had had nothing to do with the kidnaping, so the plan would have failed even if the unarmed chief had not managed to escape. He soon secured white hostages of his own. The official army records state Cochise grew so irrational that he killed his hostages, which prompted the local officers to kill his family, a war crime under any circumstance. The Apache version seems more logical, especially given their well-known regard for the lives of their family and tribesmen. The Apache claimed they had taken the whites only to exchange them for their own people. When they neared the army camp, they discovered the army had already slain them. Only then did Cochise hang his hostages. He chose the same tree where his own people had been slain. The war that followed was merciless. A sergeant sympathetic to Cochise and a supporter of the Apache version of the incident said that during that spring alone, Cochise personally burned alive thirteen whites, tortured five others by cutting pieces out of their bodies, and dragged fifteen others to death after tying a lariat around their necks. The sergeant commented sadly, "This Indian was at peace until betrayed and wounded by white men."

When the Civil War caused the Union to withdraw many troops for battles in the East, the Apache, like other Indians in the West, thought their resistance had finally weakened the whites. When various units of Confederate and Union troops appeared in the area, the Apache attacked them vigorously, hoping to drive out the divided white tribes completely. Different bands under various head men such as Cochise fought under the general but loose leadership of Magnas Coloradas, a war chief who proved to be an elusive enemy for the whites. Massacres, cruelty, and treachery on the part of whites and Apache alike during this period surpass the ferocity of anything previously experienced in the wars with Indians. At last the army sent a messenger to Magnas Coloradas in 1863, guaranteeing him safe conduct if he came to talk peace. When the chief accepted, he was captured, tortured, and "shot while trying to escape."

Cochise and his two thousand Chiricahua continued to struggle. Eventually they took possession of an impregnable mountain area they called the Stronghold. Campaigns to take Cochise were futile, but by 1872 the aging chief hoped to establish a permanent peace for his people. Tom Jeffords, a tall athletic man whom the Indians called Red Beard, proved to be the key figure in the settlement. He had had the respect and friendship of the Chiricahua ever since he had had the courage to come to the Stronghold unarmed to bargain a right of way for a stagecoach line. Now, Jeffords wanted to bring General Howard into the Stronghold for a peace parley.

When the two chiefs met, the general promised Cochise a large reservation some miles distant where all the Apache bands could be together. Cochise refused Howard's offer because he did not think the various Apache could live in peace with each other. Furthermore, he knew the army would never be able to control American civilians even if it wanted to, any more than he could control his own hotter bloods. Without the Stronghold, the Chiricahua would surely perish. Nevertheless he called in all his captains for their opinions. They decided that a reservation was acceptable, provided it was the Stronghold they now ruled. With their many well-armed braves under their own leaders in places they had known since birth, they could resist vastly superior forces. Even the very rocks were good friends who would protect them from bullets. Howard hesitated about letting Cochise have the Stronghold but the chief insisted, just as he insisted that Jeffords must be his agent, an honor Jeffords would just as soon have declined. The army was skeptical about Howard's bargain but decided to go along and the war arrows were broken.

Jeffords was an army captain at the time of the signing but the Apache were less impressed by his rank than by his genuine sense of justice. His dealings with the Chiricahua were always honorable and as long as Cochise lived there was no more fighting. Jeffords was under no illusions regarding the Apache character. He knew Cochise drank too much. He knew the chief sometimes beat his wives. He understood that Cochise was the same mixture of good and evil that all men are. The image of the blood-savoring savage was quite as false as that of the denatured, desexed Noble Savage of the missionaries and idealistic philosophers.

Just a few months before his death, Cochise had mellowed to a point where he allowed Mexicans to cross his reservation to trade, but he forbade them to cross with weapons as they had done on an earlier illegal trip. Cochise ordered rather than begged. He spoke with the authority earned as head man of the council of the Chiricahua Apache and he died exercising the full democratic power of his responsible position. The night before his death, Cochise sent for Jeffords. The old chief wanted a farewell talk with his younger friend. General Howard himself had stated that Cochise deployed men as skillfully as any officer the general had ever seen. But now, knowing that he was about to die, the chief's thoughts were on other matters. The Indians rarely quarreled about religion and each man thought of the hereafter in his own terms. Cochise said he had been dwelling on the problem of death and he had decided that an afterlife existed and that Jeffords would be there to share it with him. The categories of Indian and non-Indian were erased that night as two men talked of the ancient mysteries by the light of burning wood. The sympathy that bound them was something that could have arisen between their nations. The Indian often demonstrated he was ready to ride such a trail but the whites shunned such a road from their first steps upon what they arrogantly called a virgin continent. They continued to shun the road until long after they had finally succeeded in placing every red tribe upon a reservation.

Of the many commanders who fought against them, the Apache respected General Crook above all others. He had come to command in 1872 after a treacherous massacre of the Apache at Camp Grant the year before. Crook was an unspectacular soldier who employed basic strategy with a concern for each particular situation. His first preparation for fighting the Apache was to train small mobile columns supplied with the best mule trains available. Crook also made it a practice to hire Indian scouts and during his year in the Southwest he employed some five hundred Apache at the same pay as regular soldiers. The Apache were allowed their own war leaders who served as sergeants. These were often the best units to use against rival bands of Apache. The policy of making Apache warriors soldiers was obviously more sensible than trying to force them to be farmers, but the Indian Bureau wanted to have all Indians on reservations and it wanted all reservation Indians to be farmers.

Crook's success among the Apache led him to be promoted to commander of the entire region surrounding the Platte River in the North. As soon as Crook departed from Apache country, a foolish policy was adopted which concentrated all the Apache upon a few dry and cheerless reservations. Often groups more hostile to each other than to whites were placed on the same reservation. The situation could only result in new rebellions, and when they occurred they were as fierce as the ones Crook had helped to end. The new Apache head man was Victorio, whose band of never more than one hundred warriors killed one hundred United States soldiers, two hundred United States civilians, and two hundred Mexicans. Victorio campaigned from 1877–80 before being killed by Mexicans.

Reservation life would have been difficult for the Apache under any circumstance, but the Indian Bureau seemed to go out of its way to create trouble. The Department of the Interior had been created in 1849 and the Indian Bureau had been transferred to it from the War Department, although the War Department also continued to have power to deal with the Indians. After 1879, the Indian Bureau adopted a rigid policy of destroying everything that was distinctly Indian, especially Indian religion, language, and social habits. On many occasions, high-ranking military officers in actual contact with Indians had a better apprecia-

tion and sensitivity for their culture than the civilians of
the Indian Bureau. The civilians tended to have special interests regarding Indians. They sometimes wanted to convert them to specific Christian churches and quite often
they simply wanted to cheat them of supplies and land.

The Apache got particularly bad treatment because of
their reputations as incorrigible fighters. No livestock was
delivered to them. No effort was made to employ them in
the manner Crook had. Tribes who had feuds with one another had to share the same land. Various groups were
shuffled from place to place without their consent and
without any apparent reason. Victorio's break was seen as
inevitable, and, as the inevitable will, it happened again
and again. The new rebels were motivated by two things:
they wanted to live the exciting life of the past and they
feared the whites would kill them during their periodic fits
of violence. The most important of the new rebels was Geronimo, a warrior who had fought under Magnas Colorados and Cochise.

Geronimo's legend is spectacular, but his exploits were
neither high-minded nor inspiring. He was not a Pontiac or
a Tecumseh with a vision of uniting the Indians. Geronimo was simply a marauder, a marauder of the sort the
Apache had always been. He was concerned with keeping
his band as safe and prosperous as possible. He was neither
more nor less cruel, more nor less cunning, more nor less
set in his ways than most other Apache head men. Like
other bands, his men knew the land so well that a few
stones out of place would give them important information.
They were able to walk seventy-five miles a day in the hot-
test deserts. They signaled to each other with sudden puffs
of smoke in graceful clouds to let their comrades know
strange parties were approaching. Rapidly multiplying
clouds meant the travelers were well armed, and steady

smoke meant the band should collect at some prearranged place for joint action. At night the flames of a fire set on a high mesa could be used the same way.

The campaigns of Geronimo were filled with murder, but the treachery he had personally experienced was rarely mentioned by his white enemies. Geronimo had lost his mother, his wife, and three children in an unprovoked Mexican raid. He knew that almost two hundred Apache women and children had been killed at the Camp Grant Massacre. He knew that an army officer had cut off the head of Magnas Colorados and sent it east as a curiosity. He knew how the war with Cochise had begun. He always claimed that the reason he left the reservations so many times was that the whites were always threatening to jail or kill him.

General Crook was called to Apache country in 1882 in hopes that he could renew his successes against the Indians. His first move was to organize a new corps of scouts. Within a short time, he was able to cross into Mexico and enter the Sierre Madre camp of Geronimo. The talk between the two chiefs went well. Geronimo agreed to return to the San Carlos reservation once he gathered up his scattered families. Some Apache returned immediately with Crook, and weeks later Geronimo himself turned up with a stolen herd of cattle of over three hundred head. Crook was severely criticized for his handling of the wily Geronimo by government officials who wanted quick decisive defeats. They did not understand Geronimo was acting in the proper Apache fashion in providing his people with cattle, just as Geronimo did not understand why Crook took away those cattle. The officials also did not understand that Crook's honorable manner of dealing with Apache was the best if not the only way to prevent new outbreaks.

There is good evidence that Geronimo tried to be a farmer after his first surrender to Crook. Unfortunately, the newspapers played up his former raids in sensational stories. Dishonest political forces in Tucson were anxious for more Indian trouble, and there was continual arguing over policy between the army and the Indian Bureau. By the spring of 1885 the tensions on Geronimo became too great for him to bear. In later years, he would explain the cause of his outbreak:

> I was living peaceably with my family, having plenty to eat, sleeping well, taking care of my people, perfectly contented. I don't know where those bad stories first came from. There we were, doing well and being well. I was behaving well. I hadn't killed a horse or a man, American or Indian. I don't know what was the matter with the people in charge of us. They knew this to be so, and yet they said I was a bad man and the worst man there; but what harm had I done? I was living peaceably and well, but I did not leave on my own accord. Had I left it would have been right to blame me; but as it is, blame those men who started this talk about me.

What followed was a year and a half of violent marauding, sometimes with luck, sometimes with hard times, but always with death. The size of the band was never the same, the braves came and left whenever they wished. The Mexicans and Americans pursued with great determination, but Geronimo might have stayed out indefinitely had not many of his people become lonesome for their relatives at San Carlos. One of his half brothers wanted to surrender in order to be with his wife again. Other brothers said they did not want him to go in alone.

A peace was almost accomplished about a year after the outbreak. General Crook again managed to get word to

Geronimo about a peace conference. The two leaders, accompanied by their warriors, met at Canyon de los Embudos in northern Mexico from March 25 to March 27. A photographer took pictures so that "the folks back East" could see what the mighty Geronimo looked like. The chief agreed to return to San Carlos but that very night a smuggler sold him liquor and Geronimo bolted with a third of his band, leaving seventy-seven Apache to be taken as prisoners of war.

Crook was again criticized for his handling of the matter and he asked to be relieved of his command. His successor was General Miles who was ordered to pursue and destroy the hostile Indians while making maximum use of regular troops. This direct policy statement implied criticism of the use of Apache scouts, who some bureaucrats thought were in league with Geronimo. Miles had an additional two thousand men assigned to him, bringing his command to a full five thousand soldiers. Miles also had use of the heliograph, a new wireless telegraphic device involving mirrors. This gadget had just been perfected by the signal corps to co-ordinate the movement of troops over wide areas. The general campaigned with all his energy and skill but during four vigorous months in the field, neither he, nor his heliographic corps, nor his five thousand men could kill or capture a single Apache.

When word arrived that Geronimo was again willing to negotiate, Miles sent a lieutenant and two Apache scouts to investigate. Geronimo was being hard pressed by the Mexicans and wanted to surrender to the United States. His band had been fluctuating as usual. His top strength had been thirty-five warriors with about one hundred women and children. When he actually surrendered he had two dozen men and fourteen women and children with him. During his time off the reservation he had only lost six men and four women while killing ten bluecoats, twelve Indian scouts, seventy-five United States civilians, and one hundred Mexicans.

Geronimo's surrender in September 1886 was turned into a catastrophe for the entire Chiricahua people for they were all shipped to Florida as incorrigible prisoners of war. All the Chiricahua were sent whether they had remained on the reservation or had fought, whether they were warriors, old men, women, or infants. Even the two scouts who had risked their lives to arrange the surrender were imprisoned. The racist assumptions behind Indian policy had never been so blatantly exposed. The toll in

The legendary Geronimo is third from the right in the front row of these Apache prisoners being shipped to Florida by train. (*National Archives*)

sickness and death took its place beside the Cherokee Trail of Tears and the Navajo Long Walk.

The Apache were kept in Florida until 1894 when they were transferred to Oklahoma where they were kept under guard until 1914. Geronimo survived the various movings and diseases and proved to be far less incorrigible than the Indian haters had claimed. He eventually took part in the inaugural parade of President Theodore Roosevelt and was a charmer who sold his autograph at regional and world fairs. The tough raider who had terrorized Americans and Mexicans for forty years even converted to Christianity, joining the Dutch Reformed Church in 1903. Geronimo had always been a heavy drinker, and it was the white man's whiskey which finally ended his life. One night while riding back from town in a drunken stupor, the eighty-year-old Geronimo fell from his seat and cracked open his skull upon his own wagon.

The Apache were as wild as the Pueblo were mystical, but their wildness partly sprang from an unrestrained love of personal freedom. The tale of Massai exhibits Apache exuberance at its best. He was a warrior who had fought with Geronimo at times and lived on a reservation at other times. When the Chiricahua were being packed into box-cars for shipment to Florida he urged a final uprising. Failing to convince the others, he sat quietly until one night in the middle of Kansas he jumped from the train. He had no idea of where he was. He could only travel at night. He could ask no one for help or directions. But he found his way back to the very place where he was born. Soon he stole a Mescalero woman and took her with him to the mountains where he lived another twenty-five years in absolute freedom.

The same spirit infused a handful of Chiricahua and

some San Carlos Apache who had not come in with Geronimo but stayed in Old Mexico as a distinct group until at least the 1930s. Geronimo's cousin became a Presbyterian and eagerly took up the ways of the whites, but he always defended his people. He knew full well the contrast between the way Indians treated one another and the way whites treated one another. He warned his white fellow citizens:

> You white people can now go about your business without fear of attack by Apaches. But you are still subject to being preyed upon. Beware of your own race, who are seeking an easy path to wealth at your expense.

Part II

Ishi, last of the Yahi Indians of California. (*Lowie Museum of Anthropology, University of California, Berkeley*)

Where the Sun Falls into the Sea:
CALIFORNIA

You stay, I go

Epitaph of Ishi, Last of the Yahi

California Tribes

DEATH IN THE MISSIONS

California was the golden temptress of the frontier where
the worst and best aspects of the West mingled freely like
so many drinkers at a common bar. Even before the whites
came, the area had been a mixture of different tribes living
in patterns unlike the tribes of the Atlantic coast. The
land was so bountiful that almost every migratory group
passing through had left some part of its people to settle
permanently. There were forty major groups speaking at
least twenty languages with five hundred smaller divisions
having a hundred dialects. At the time of the Spanish con-
quest over a hundred and fifty thousand Indians lived in
California, making it one of the most densely populated
regions in all of North America. Food was so abundant
and the climate so favorable that loosely organized tribes
had little experience with wars, social unrest, or depriva-
tions. They were little given to fighting in any form and
rarely moved from their traditional gathering grounds.
Hospitality was their personal and national rule. Material
wealth was accumulated for the pleasure of giving. Mystic
religions and poetic rituals provided a rich ceremonial life
from birth to death.

The Californians were simple people. Early travelers reported that they were birdlike even to their twittering
speech and the bright colors with which they painted their
bodies and possessions. The first visitors were greeted by

canoes of singing Indians who came to see the bearded men who wore metal. They danced and played music for the newcomers. They had no fear of the whites and did everything they knew to make the strangers happy.

The life ways of Californians were determined primarily by the excellent climate and the fertile soil of their region. Acorns which were ground to meal and several types of corn could be had for the gathering, and provided the base for any number of tasty dishes. Flour was made from bitter plums. Roots, berries, nuts, greens, currants, small game, and the inexhaustible bounty of the sea added variety to a tribe's feasting. Rabbits were particularly plentiful and whatever was not available locally could be obtained by trading over sea or land.

The Californians lived out of doors most of the time, moving from one favored gathering place to another while carefully observing rigid tribal boundaries. When they required shelter, the Indians dug a hole about two feet deep and erected a hut of bush and bark supported on crisscrossed poles. They walked barefoot and wore few if any clothes although they liked to tattoo and paint themselves extensively. Some women covered their entire upper bodies with fine lattice patterns that gave the illusion of an intricately woven garment. Shells and unusual rocks were used by both sexes to make necklaces, earrings, combs, and arm bands.

The tribelets gathered or fished in small groups under the leadership of a head man and his council. The leader usually had a sacred hut or carried a "magic bundle" consisting of skins or feathers of creatures he had seen in a vision or found near a place where he had had a vision. The leader was always a good singer who knew the creation myths from beginning to end and generally, he was an expert in the eagle dance. The chiefs had few civil decisions to make as there was little to quarrel about. Children were never punished and there were few crimes. The one act that aroused indignation and carried the death penalty was when an individual used up food that had been gathered for the use of all. Feasts and dances were common, with puberty a special time for males and females. The boys' elaborate initiation rites included the use of the dangerous Jimson weed which was supposed to help the youths secure visions. Marriage came in late adolescence and men with more than one wife were common. Divorce was a simple matter with the female returning to her parent's home and both parties easily securing new mates.

Strangely enough, the happy singers to whom so much had been given were the Indians who thought most about death. Their dead were cremated, and elaborate mourning procedures were required one year after the cremation. Some tribes placed the ashes of the dead in exquisite jars which rivaled their baskets in beauty and grace. The Yuma, who lived on the deserts bordering the Colorado River, developed the death phobia to its fullest degree. They did not have the elaborate rituals of the corn-growing pueblo dwellers. Rather than being concerned with the powers that control rain, Yuma creation myths were pessimistic and dealt with a dying god. Different versions of the myth had the god becoming the first cremation and his son or brother continuing the work of making the Colorado River and holy places. The California tribes tended to be less extreme in their beliefs, but they had the same basic viewpoint. In one legend, the god Wiyot knew his daughter would poison him. Each month he would ask, "Shall I die this month?"

The Spanish missionaries who established their first churches in 1769 sought to erase the death religions with their promise of resurrection, but they ended by playing the daughter to the Californian's Wiyot. Legends of a lost tribe of white brothers aided the padres in making their first converts as the Indians flocked to accept the magic of the gray robes and to marvel at the strength and beauty of the new places of worship. The Franciscans brought grapes, plums, olives, oranges, carrots, lettuce, and cabbage as well as new tools such as the plow, hoe, pick, and spade. The Indians were fascinated by all the new things but they soon discovered the Spanish would not allow them to live as they had in the past. The Indians were forced to settle within the mission walls, and soldiers made certain they did not run away. If an Indian attempted to escape, he was tracked down and punished severely. The Christian fathers had pledged lives of poverty and industry, but they made the Indians work hard to create the wealth that enabled the Franciscan order to extend its missions up the entire California coast. Indians worked that soldiers could be well fed and comfortable. Once they had been able to get all they needed by simply taking it from the earth. Now, they labored all day to earn a pint of corn.

Men and women who had always lived in freedom were locked in the mission compounds from nine in the evening until morning prayers. The people who had enjoyed nudity were forced to wear pants, skirts, shoes, and shirts. Any who dared rebel were whipped or placed in stocks or shackled. The Californians had never known punishment yet now their women might be locked in stocks for three days and their men lashed until blood ran down their backs. The Indians had been possessed with thoughts of death and now death became their constant, often welcomed, comrade. Mothers sometimes chose to smother their newborn rather than subject them to mission life.

When Mexico won independence from Spain all aid to the missions was cut off. The last mission was built in 1832 and two summers later economic collapse shattered the

Franciscan empire. The Indians had been wrenched from their traditional ways yet they had never been allowed to integrate into the new. Their hearts had long been broken and now their bodies could not resist the starvation, despondency, and diseases which swept the compounds. By 1880 there would be fewer than twenty thousand Indians in all of California and half of those would be reservation hostages from other states.

The missionaries were so zealous in spreading Catholicism that they ignored the ancient lore of the people they sought to convert. Rich Indian cultures passed into oblivion without any effort to preserve their languages, traditions, and religions. The ecological balance which had been developed over hundreds of years perished under the well-meaning but stern Franciscan heel. Even the economic collapse of 1834 would have been far less disastrous if the Indians had not already been psychologically destroyed. Their imaginative spirit and colorful life had been torn from them in a manner whose thoroughness was matched only by its speed. Only a single lifetime separated the ways of the centuries from the shattered refugees of the mission compounds. Californians were folk of the dance and song. They were the spontaneous, the unfettered. Disease, murder, exploitation, and economic depression destroyed them in a way unprecedented even in the United States.

The greed of the Gold Rush was the final seal on the Indian coffin. The padres had desired to help the Indians, the miners of 1849 wished only to destroy them. The U. S. Government encouraged rather than restrained its citizens in their Indian hatred. During the first years of the 1850s, treaties were negotiated with hundreds of tribes residing in the best parts of the state. The agreements deprived the Indians of almost all their lands, but still the California whites thought the treaties were much too generous. Their representatives in Washington were so powerful that the United States Senate refused to ratify the treaties. The Indian Bureau had never been noted for its integrity and after the political death of the treaties, the bureau lived up to its bad reputation by consciously adopting a policy of open deception. The bureau simply failed to inform the Indians that the treaties had been rejected by the Great Council of the whites. The honest tribesmen abided by their agreements only to have the white government sell every acre of land promised to them.

Little is known of the cultures that were snuffed out so quickly. The objects that do survive suggest that the Californians may have been among the most interesting of all the Indian nations, certainly the most delightful. The women of the Pomo in central California were so skillful at weaving that a microscope is needed to see their individual stitches. Colored designs were improved by working in the brilliant feathers of birds such as woodpeckers and warblers. The birds also influenced Californian music. The most common instruments aside from the human voice were wooden whistles and rattles made of shells and pebbles. Music was almost always accompanied by singing or dancing. Among some tribes the shamans performed a fire dance in which they pushed hot embers into a pile with their bare feet.

California art achieved its most individual tone in a small area around what is now Santa Barbara, where a tribe called the Chumash lived. The Chumash have left eighty sites of distinctive rock paintings. Their work is not drawn lifelike, but highly stylized and semiabstract. Buglike creatures with angular bodies serve as the main features. Black, red, and white coloring predominate with an occasional sprinkling of yellow. A marvelous sense of humor and liberty infuses every line. The delightful animals have multiple legs, pinwheel heads, and tails that look like exploding fireworks. The paintings range from being several inches long to huge efforts covering more than forty feet of cave wall. Some are simple line drawings and others are full paintings. They were pecked, cut, and rubbed on cavern walls. The Chumash loved to paint whatever they could—their faces, their bodies, their weapons, their few clothes. Their canoes were bathed in red and colored boards marked their burial places. The joyful rock paintings inspire the viewer to know more of the people who made them. But there is no one left to speak of them. The California tribes were too gentle to survive white civilization. They were like the eagle of one of their myths who sang:

> At the time of death
> when I found there was to be death,
> I was very much surprised.
> All was failing.
> My home,
> I was sad to leave it.
>
> I have been looking far,
> sending my spirit north, south, east, and west
> trying to escape death
> but could find nothing.
> No way to escape.

CAPTAIN JACK

Few of the Californians knew how to fight back against the whites, but one small group humiliated the United States army in a fashion unique in the Indian wars. In a struggle lasting almost half a year a handful of poorly equipped Modoc warriors held off an entire army. Their successes indicate how much damage the Indians might have done had their notions of war and honor been different than they were.

The Modoc bands had done some raiding and fighting in the 1850s but the whites had retaliated with so many soldiers and massacres that the tribe had agreed to a reservation. They took up the white man's clothing and habits, and they tried to live in peace. The only other Indians who spoke the same language happened to be the Klamath, who lived just north of them in Oregon. In its usual disregard for Indian feuds, the Indian Bureau placed the Modoc and Klamath on the same reservation. The inevitable quarrels broke out and several Modoc groups left the reservation to return to their old homes along Lost River.

On November 28, 1872, thirty-eight soldiers were dispatched to bring in the band of Kintpuash (known to the whites as Captain Jack because of his fondness for bits and pieces of military uniforms and paraphernalia). The Modoc had not left the reservation on a whim and they resisted the troops sent to take them back. The soldiers retreated to get reinforcements and the band headed for a place they called Land-of-Burnt-out-Fires, an area of lava beds. The wild jumble of caverns and ridges made the land look like a hard sponge. One section called the Stronghold was surrounded by chasms that formed natural trench systems, which made the higher ground like a fortified castle. A few parts of the lava beds were fertile and provided enough water and game for the small band of perhaps 120 Modoc. Within a short time an additional group from Hot Creek under the leadership of Curly Headed Doctor and Hooker Jim joined the band of Captain Jack. The total

From caves such as this one in the middle of rugged lava beds, the Modoc followers of Captain Jack were able to hold off U.S. soldiers for months. (*National Archives*)

combined warrior strength was never more than fifty but the fortresslike terrain gave the Modoc strength far beyond their numbers.

A large body of troops arrived at the lava beds in early January. The soldiers attempted to assault the Modoc positions in a traditional frontal attack, but the Indians had learned every twist of every ridge and had prepared special vantage points for their fighting men. White casualties mounted at a rapid rate with no Modoc being seen, much less injured or captured. Bullets and howitzer shells uselessly ricocheted off rocks and were more dangerous to those who fired them than to their Modoc targets. The Indians were made even more confident when they saw that no soldier was able to pass beyond the magic line drawn by Curly Headed Doctor.

Repeated attempts to take the lava beds were equally futile, and the army sent word that it wanted to negotiate. Captain Jack was willing to take a reservation as long as it was separate from the Klamath, but men like Hooker Jim and Curly Headed Doctor had other fears. They had committed crimes of robbery and murder and thought the whites would punish them if they surrendered. Captain Jack stated his dilemma as chief of the rebels:

> I want to go and see my people on the reservation. My mind is made up to say "yes." I have a good heart, and want no mistake made this time, to live with good heart and talk truth. I have no paper men, and can't write on paper. The papers called me bad and lied about me. If they don't lie to me, I won't lie to them. I want to give up shooting . . . I wish to live like the whites. Let everything be wiped out, washed out, and let there be no more blood. I have got a bad heart about those murderers. I have got but a few men and I don't see how I can give them up. Will they give up their people who murdered my people while they were asleep? . . . I can see how I could give up my horse to be hanged; but I can't see how I could give up my men to be hanged. I could give up my horse to be hanged and I wouldn't cry about it; but if I gave up my men I would have to cry about it. I want them all to have good hearts now. I have thrown everything away. There must be no more bad talk. I will not. I have spoken forever. I want soldiers all to go home. I have given up now and want no more fuss. I have said yes and thrown away my country. I want soldiers to go away so I will not be afraid.

The one thing that was certain was that the soldiers

would not go away. Their defeat had not affected their
confidence but it had injured their pride. A peace commission began to meet with the Modoc leaders in Feb-
ruary. Its leadership soon fell to Brigadier General Canby,
commander of the entire region. The Modoc retained
their strong military positions and their previous victories
meant they were able to bargain from strength. They
were amazed and insulted to discover the army came not
to discuss but to dictate. Canby presented a series of
demands. Jack was annoyed. "I will not agree on anything
you may offer until you agree to give me a home in my
native country." Jack asked for a specific place long
wanted as a reservation by the Modoc but he said his
men might settle for the lava beds to show their reason-
ableness. The army responded that it couldn't take up the
matter of a reservation, that reservations were civilian, not
military matters. Canby even pressed the Modoc leadership on the question of unpunished criminals who were
fighting with Jack. The chief again answered that he
was willing to give up his accused men for white trial
whatever day the whites chose to give up their men who
were accused of murdering Modoc women for Indian
trial. Reverend Thomas, another member of the negotiat-
ing commission, told Jack that he must place more trust
in God. Jack countered that he trusted the spirits very
much but that unfortunately he was not dealing with the
spirits but with soldiers wearing blue cloth and brass buttons.

The bargaining dragged on for more than two months.
The Modoc grew more and more impatient with Jack,
and the government pressed Canby to make some agreement or resume the fighting. Some of Jack's men said he
was a coward. Others accused him of wanting to betray
them for personal gain. Curly Headed Doctor suggested

Jack could prove his bravery by killing everyone on the peace commission at a meeting. During the heat of one debate, several friends of Curly Headed Doctor snuck up behind Jack and placed a woman's headdress and female garments on him. Jack tore away the clothes angrily and shouted that if there was to be any killing he would slay Canby himself. Later he asked the council to release him from his oath. "Death is mighty bad. Death will come to us soon enough." His men would not reverse their decision and Jack agreed to go through with the pledge rather than lose leadership of the group.

At the new conference, Captain Jack repeated his position and Canby repeated his. As no compromise seemed possible Jack kept the promise he had given his followers and shot General Canby beneath the right eye. The commissioner who had wanted the Modoc to place more trust in God was also shot. Other warriors set upon two other commissioners but a Modoc woman had given them advance warning of possible trouble and the alerted men were able to escape with minor wounds. After returning to his stronghold, Jack's original doubts about the wisdom of the killings returned. He spent much of his time meditating in the cave which he used as his home.

Canby was the highest-ranking officer ever to be killed by Indians, but, of course, his murder could not possibly aid the Modoc cause. The Indians thought that killing the leader of the besieging forces would make them headless warriors who would lose heart and go home. They did not realize that the United States army had a hundred generals and that the pony soldiers were not Indians who fought according to individual will but paid fighters who were drilled in the strictest discipline.

The shocked and angered soldiers grouped their forces to deal the Modoc a blow that would wipe them out.

Four companies of reserves were brought to the lava beds, bringing a section of twelve-pound mortars and men who could handle the weapons with better skill than the cavalrymen had. From their vantage points, eight Indians had been able to pin down four hundred soldiers. The shells had rebounded harmlessly on rocks and the magic rope of Curly Headed Doctor had not been crossed. In the new fighting the Modoc did not fare as well. The army attacked in two strong columns supported by heavy mortar and howitzer fire. They were able to gain territory and cut off the Modoc from their supply of water. The army clearly won the battle, but all the members of the band escaped capture.

The months that followed were a cycle of hide-and-seek fighting in the rocks. The army was tireless in its searching but the Modoc were just as untiring in eluding. The Modoc relied heavily on ambushes and attacking dozing sentries. They sometimes raided ranches in the area and ran off livestock for food. A typical fight occurred on April 6 when twenty-one soldiers were killed and twenty more wounded in an ambush. Even more might have died if a relief column had not been attracted by the shooting. The soldiers grew so desperate that when they found one dead Modoc warrior, they cut his scalp into a hundred pieces and even shaved off his eyebrows.

The only chance the band had was to exhaust the soldiers. They might have succeeded if arguments had not begun to split them. Curly Headed Doctor sought to convince Jack's men to fight under his leadership, but they stayed loyal to their original head man. The fourteen warriors following the medicine man often fought independently of Jack's men. At least three hundred soldiers were always in the field against the Modoc. In early May the Modoc prepared a new ambush by Dry Lake, an area of volcanic ashes. The army horses were successfully stampeded but a charge on foot broke the Modoc force into small parties. Curly Headed Doctor, Hooker Jim, and others were captured. They offered to scout against Jack if they would be shown clemency for the crimes they had committed before the outbreak of the miniature war. The army agreed for, as long as Jack was free, the Modoc would continue to fight. The individual who had been taunted for being a coward proved to have the strongest will and bravest spirit while his tormentors became traitors. When the turncoats approached Jack about surrendering, he spat out his defiance and refused to talk with them. Some of Jack's followers talked for a time with the turncoats but no agreement was possible. A few of the Modoc families slipped back to the reservation making a *de facto* peace of their own. Jack regretted the killing of Canby, and the life of constant war oppressed his spirit. Food was scarce and water was particularly difficult to get. Life had become an endless hunt with Jack the chief prey. Hooker Jim and others led the army to where Jack was camped. He might have escaped but Modoc disunity and the idea of once more fleeing at last broke him. His statement upon surrender was blunt. "My legs have given out."

The members of the band were treated as prisoners of war, but the six individuals who were responsible for the actual murdering of the peace commissioners were held as criminals. A trial was convened under the white man's law and the death verdict duly arrived at. Jack's good humor and no nonsense attitude stayed with him to the end. When he was told by a well-meaning minister that he was going to a better place than anything on earth, Jack offered the minister the privilege of taking his place. He added he would throw in all his horses as a bonus.

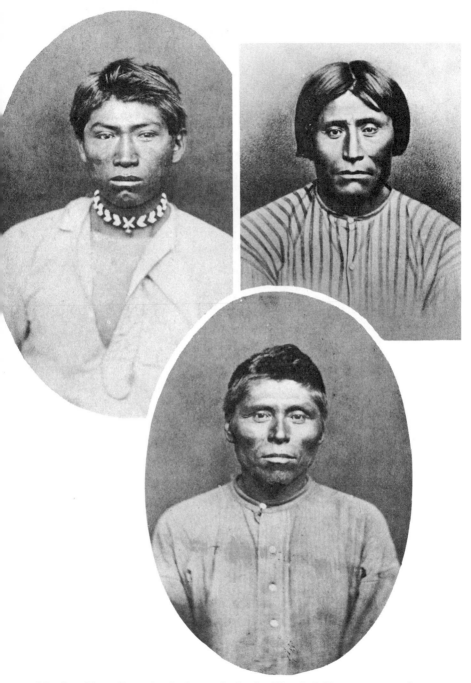

Hooker Jim, Captain Jack, and Curly Headed Doctor were the leaders of the Modoc war in 1873. (*National Archives*)

The army had decided that it must warn other tribes from the path chosen by the Modoc. A well-publicized execution was thought to be a good policy. The newly elected President Grant decided to commute the sentence of two of the condemned to imprisonment because both the Indians and the military considered the youths to be below average intelligence and not fully responsible for their actions. But his mercy was kept secret until the very moment of execution on October 3, 1873, when Captain Jack and three others were hanged. The story of the Modoc resistance and the subsequent hangings swept the Indian nations. Rather than closing an era of conflict, the Modoc campaign was a prelude to a new series of wars. The policy of intimidation by execution proved to have the opposite effect. Chiefs who might have surrendered thought it best to continue fighting because they feared they would share the fate of Captain Jack.

The reservation the Modoc had desired consisted of two thousand acres and was valued at no more than twenty thousand dollars. The lava beds they would have taken as a substitute were worth considerably less. The American government had not been generous enough to grant the modest Modoc request. The final cost had been the death of a brigadier general, seven officers, thirty-nine privates, sixteen volunteers, two scouts, and eighteen civilians in a war costing more than half a million dollars. The humiliation was all the greater since the Modoc lost only five warriors, two of whom died examining an unexploded shell after a battle. The Modoc resistance was an affair the army wanted to forget as rapidly as possible. A magician more gifted than Curly Headed Doctor was needed to justify the bloody folly.

ISHI, LAST OF THE YAHI

One of the headlines of 1911 carried the astounding story of the discovery of a living "prehistoric" man in California. The individual was a starved Indian who had staggered into the corral of a slaughter house. His hair had been burned off close to his scalp and his only clothing was a ragged canvas cape. He would eat and drink nothing during his first days among the whites. Deer thongs hung from his ears and a wooden plug was in the septum of his nose. Somehow a man from the Neolithic Age seemed to have stumbled into the twentieth century.

Attempts to communicate with the wild man were useless. Indians tried various tribal dialects and Mexicans employed different Spanish idioms but there was no response. The strange man might have remained in his frenzied isolation until death had it not been for Albert Kroeber of the University of California. Kroeber was an expert on the California tribes and he knew of stories concerning a wild group of Yahi people belonging to the Yana nation. The professor visited the jail where the Indian was being held. He brought along a list of Yana words and then began to pronounce them one by one. The strange man listened intently but seemed to understand nothing until half way through the list Kroeber pronounced the word for wood correctly. The Indian's eyes glowed as if he had been recalled from the dead. He pointed to the wood of his cot and repeated *siwini*. From that first word a friendship developed that would endure for the rest of the Indian's life and would reveal one of the most pathetic stories concerning the white assault on Native Americans.

The Yana people, made up of three to four thousand people, lived in a mountainous region of California. The Yahi subgroup to which the man of 1911 belonged had about four hundred warriors. All the Indians of America had watched the wagons moving westward, but the Yana in California were among those who received the brunt of land-hungry settlers who had crossed a continent of miles to build new lives. Many of the Yana lived in backwater regions, but their remoteness did not save them. The best lands were soon taken and the whites sought any fertile spot even if it were not of the first quality. Adding to the difficulties of the Yana was the aggressive spirit of the settlers. Land counted for everything and Indian rights were nothing. Many of the men who arrived during the period of the Gold Rush were frustrated by the lack of women, by corruption, and by the failure to make an instant fortune. Desperation of every variety flourished and the Yana were perfect scapegoats. Between 1852–67 almost all the tribesmen became virtual slaves of their white employers. Every Indian girl and woman was subjected to being assaulted repeatedly or being forced to become a prostitute. During the twenty years following the Gold Rush venereal disease infected 40 to 80 per cent of various tribes. Other diseases such as measles, chickenpox, smallpox, malaria, tuberculosis, typhoid, dysentery, influenza, and pneumonia killed off most of the Indian population.

The Yana were overwhelmed by the horrors that had

burst upon them so unexpectedly. They were a people who had no weapons as such beyond their hunting equipment. The first white man to live in their territory never saw one of them although he noticed logs they used to cross creeks and frequently spotted their footprints. The Yana did not bother the settlers but the new settlers thought any land they could hold on to with force was rightfully theirs. Desperados and toughs in saloons and bunkhouses smoldered with all the frustrations of frontier California. They found outlets for their disappointments in persecution of the Indians. Their cruelty is clearly recorded in many diaries kept by whites. The saloon gangs thought it was good sport to take Indian girls from their white employers, assault them and kill them by smashing their skulls. Yana who worked for whites were frequently stopped and robbed of their wages after being beaten unconscious. The men for whom the Indians worked were disturbed by what the hoodlums did but they would not risk their own security to save their Indian employees. The Yana began to fight back and the Yahi proved to be their most able warriors. The struggle reached its climax in the sixties when the Yahi were responsible for the death of fifty settlers.

The white response to the Indians' defense of their lives and honor was a series of massacres aimed at eventual extermination of every Yahi. The tribe retreated to living in caves and tried to avoid all contact with whites. Their birth rate fell far below the death rate as war reduced them to a fraction of their former numbers. By 1872 the tribe had decided the best way to resist was not to resist at all. They would simply vanish. The number of Yahi still alive at this time is unknown but it could not have been great or the tribe would not have been able to conceal itself so successfully. For twelve years the Yahi ceased

to exist. Their warriors stole no horses and took no supplies. Everyone was careful to leave no footprints or
damaged arrows. Ashes were scattered and campfires cun-
ningly concealed. The men fished with the noiseless har-
poon and net; they hunted with the silent bow and arrow;
and they trapped with the voiceless snare. The Indians
avoided known paths and scaled canyon walls using ropes
made of milkweed fiber. Their memory was erased from
the minds of whites.

The tribe had dwindled to a handful of individuals by
1884 and the last adult hunter had died. Hunger never
left them. The band was forced to take greater risks as
new roads and ranches penetrated into the most distant
regions. The survivors slaughtered a few calves and stole
some sheep to fight off starvation. They robbed cabins of
flour and uncanned food. Most whites assumed the thieves
to be outlaws or adolescents, but in 1885 four Yahi were
seen by a settler as they attempted to steal from one of
his cabins. The man described the Indians as a young
woman, an old man, and two young boys, one crippled.
The settler had a rifle and could have taken all four as
prisoners but he was so moved by their pathetic condition
that he waved them away with hopes for good fortune.
The Indians were on the brink of starvation at this time
yet they were so grateful for the unusual kindness that
later in the year the man returned to the cabin to find
two beautiful Indian baskets had been left for him upon
the table.

In 1894 the raids ended once more as the remnant of
no more than a dozen Indians retreated to an area near
Deer Creek. The survivors soon dwindled to a family of five
headed by the man who came to be known as Ishi. The
family was always cautious that the whites should not see
them or follow their trail. Ishi had been a fugitive all his

life. He had never yet known a woman and never would. He never knew the routine of normal Indian life and never would. He never knew the happiness of tribal living and never would. He had been victimized as few American Indians had. Yet Ishi loved the things of nature and would have been content if the whites had allowed his small family to live in peace.

Legends about the wild Yahi persisted but they seemed to have no basis in fact until a settler's cabin was broken into in 1906. Definite proof that the Indians actually existed came two years later when the naked Ishi, now in his thirties, was seen by two men as he fished in a stream with his spear. A group of whites went looking for the hunter and came upon the cabins the five had lived in for so long. Ishi's wrinkled and white-haired mother was found under a pile of skins. Her semiparalyzed legs were swollen. Rather than moving the whites to compassion, the dying woman's condition disgusted them. They took all the food and other things of value in the cabin and left. One of them was so ashamed of his conduct that he returned the next day only to find the woman had disappeared.

Ishi had seen the party of whites and had hidden himself. His sister, carrying an old man on her back, had moved through the woods toward some hiding places near Deer Creek. After the whites had finished their ransacking Ishi carried his mother to another refuge where she died just a few days later. Ishi searched for his sister everywhere but he was never to see her or the old man again. He imagined they had drowned in the creek or been eaten by a bear or mountain lion. For the next three years, from November 1908 to August 1911, Ishi lived alone. His diet grew worse and worse. His spirit sank. He felt death calling so chose to burst dramatically upon the whites, half

Ishi was teacher as well as student of the scholars who befriended him. (*Courtesy of Museum of the American Indian, Heye Foundation*)

wishing they would quickly put an end to the last of the Yahi.

The anthropologist who befriended Ishi at the jail took him to the Berkeley Museum in the "iron horse" Ishi's mother had said was a demon. At Berkeley, Ishi regained his health and came to know the men with whom he would share the remaining years of his life. The white professors were excited by the living history Ishi represented, but they also came to regard him as a personal friend. Ishi was given a room in the museum and he performed custodial tasks to earn money since no funds were given to him by the government or university in spite of the decades of brutalization the whites had subjected him to. Actually, Ishi was glad to work. He found everything in the white world new. The tools of the janitor were easier for him to cope with than the complex wonders of a twentieth-century city.

Men less idealistic than Kroeber and his colleague Thomas Waterman might have exploited Ishi as a cheap sideshow amusement, but the professors were of the best breed of whites. They developed their friend's self-esteem and confidence in whatever way they could. Ishi proved to have a generous soul and a quick mind. The learned anthropologists regarded him as a teacher as well as a student. Ishi understood the mutual nature of their relationship. He spent many of his days talking with them of Indian things or visiting with Dr. Pope, the university physician, who became one of his best friends. At specific hours, Ishi gave demonstrations of Indian lore to museum guests. Again, what might have become a sick spectacle was handled with such propriety that the children and adults who visited Ishi became appreciative learners rather than gawkers. Many of them returned frequently and some even corresponded with him from distant states.

Ishi enjoyed the enthusiasm of the whites, especially the children.

Ishi learned to use about six hundred English words and could carry on fairly complex conversations. He went about the city by himself and took trips with various friends. His reactions were often unpredictable. When taken to plays, he was more fascinated by the many whites sitting quietly row after row than by the entertainment on the stage. In 1914 a camping trip was made to the area around Deer Creek. At first, Ishi was filled with dread at the idea of returning to the place that had meant so much poverty and terror for him, but once back in the land he had grown to manhood in, his mood shifted. He felt happy to be close to nature once more and he demonstrated the ways his people had lived to the other men in the group. His confidence in his friends grew with each passing moon. He felt freer to tell more of his personal and tribal history. Many of his previous notions and taboos gave way before the common sense he found in what the whites taught. One thing he never revealed, however, was his true name. Ishi means man in Yana. Kroeber devised the name when pestered by newsmen about what to call him. The Indians of California were very reluctant to tell their names, for it conferred power over them to those who knew it. Ishi grew close to his white friends and probably would have told them his true name in time but as it was he died before such a confidence could be reached.

Ishi's grasp of the modern world progressed at a remarkable rate until his development was cut short by tuberculosis which struck him in late 1915 when he was approximately fifty-five years old. His illness was prolonged and the professors did all in their power to make him as comfortable as possible. Feeling he would be simply another patient in the hospital, his friends cleared out a wing of the museum and transformed it into a bedroom. Ishi was given constant attention and never lost his good cheer. Doctor Pope was at his side when Ishi finally died on March 25, 1916. The anthropologists were concerned that their friend's religious beliefs about the sanctity of the body after death be honored. Kroeber wrote to his colleagues, "If there is any talk about the interest of science, as for me, science can go to hell. We propose to

The few California Indians who survived mission life, disease, and war developed a life style very different from the simplicity of their traditional ways. (*Courtesy of Museum of the American Indian, Heye Foundation*)

stand by our friend." The state authorities thought otherwise and overruled such sentiments in order to have Ishi's brain preserved and an autopsy performed on his body. Ishi's death left Kroeber and Waterman deeply frustrated. They had only begun to explore with Ishi the traditions and skills of his nation. They had imagined they would have the leisure of a lifetime in which to learn from their unique and irreplaceable expert. A grief-stricken Waterman was despondent for years and called Ishi, "my best friend." Dr. Pope had had a more satisfying relationship with Ishi. Although they often discussed medical science with one another, their friendship flourished best when they fished and hunted together or when they compared the lore of the whites with that of the Indian. Pope saw deeply into the meaning of his friend's life and death when he wrote:

> And so, stoic and unafraid, departed the last wild Indian of America. He closed a chapter in history. He looked upon us as sophisticated children—smart, but not wise. We know many things, and much that is false. He knew nature, which is always true. His were the qualities of character that last forever. He was kind; he had courage and self-restraint and though all had been taken from him, there was no bitterness in his heart. His soul was that of a child, his mind that of a philosopher.

Part III

Chief Joseph of the Nez Percé helped lead a long unsuccessful fight for a reservation in Idaho, his homeland. He said, "I am tired of talk that comes to nothing. It makes my heart sick when I remember all the good words and all the broken promises." (*Courtesy of Museum of the American Indian, Heye Foundation*)

No More Forever:
THE NORTHWEST

*I have only one heart. Although you
say go to another country, my heart
is not that way. I am here, and
here is where I am going to be. I
will not part with my lands. If
you come again, I will say the same
things. I will not part with my
lands.*

Unnamed Chief (Umatilla)

Northwestern Tribes

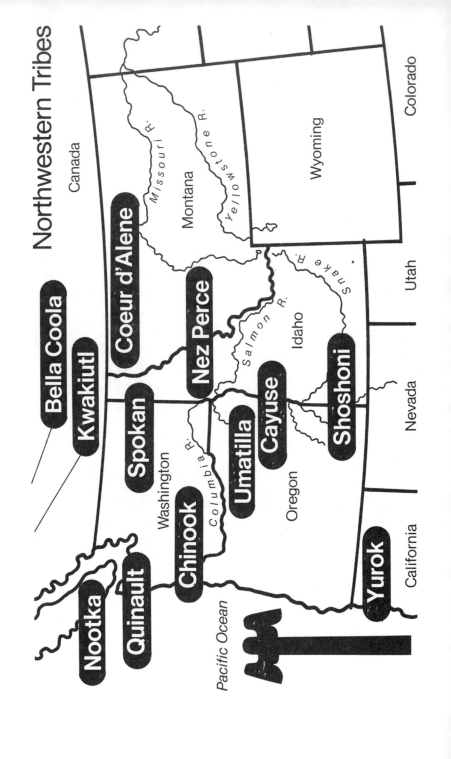

Canada

Bella Coola

Kwakiutl

Coeur d'Alene

Nootka

Quinault

Spokan

Chinook

Nez Perce

Umatilla

Cayuse

Shoshoni

Yurok

Pacific Ocean

Washington

Columbia R.

Oregon

Idaho

Salmon R.

Snake R.

Montana

Missouri R.

Yellowstone R.

Wyoming

Nevada

Utah

California

Colorado

POTLATCHERS AND TOTEM POLES

The salmon dominated the life of the Pacific Northwest as thoroughly as the buffalo dominated the life of the Great Plains. These fifteen-pound fish swimming up the rivers each summer and autumn were so numerous that early explorers bragged they could walk across the rivers on their backs. The oil-rich salmon meat was easily stored for use throughout the year and was the basic food of all tribes in the area. The ocean provided other food as well. Shellfish could be gathered on beaches, and each spring there were smelt thickly clustered on the surf. Spring also brought the oil-rich candlefish and herring which had the added advantage of leaving eggs that could be eaten at once. Farther out to sea were halibut, cod, sturgeon, sea otter, and sea lion. These fish could be taken by harpooning, spearing, dipnetting, and trapping. The Nootka of Vancouver Island even went out to the deepest waters to hunt the fifty-foot humpback whale from their rugged dugout canoes. Most important of all, however, were the salmon which sought to reproduce themselves in the quiet backwaters of the rivers emptying into the Pacific.

Like all the Indian nations, the tribes of the Pacific Northwest developed rituals to reconcile their belief in the sacredness of all life with their need to survive. They developed the idea that salmon were really spirits in special clothing. The first salmon of the year was taken by holy men and treated as a special visitor. The fish were thought to want to be caught and eaten, but their bones had to be returned to the water so that the salmon spirits could reclothe themselves for the following year. Exact rules were created for every act having to do with the salmon: catching, skinning, preparing, and eating.

The Northwest Indians were so prosperous that they developed a unique custom called the potlatch from the Nootka word *potshatl,* meaning *to give.* The potlatch was a feast in which an individual gained honor by giving away as many gifts as possible. Generosity, however, was not the motive of the gift giving, for each person who received a gift was under a strict obligation to make a return gift. Far from being a ceremony of sharing, the potlatch was an occasion for egotism and boasting which reinforced the prestige and power of the elite. The host worked hard to get acknowledgments of worth from his guests, and the guests worked hard to get gifts in keeping with what they felt they were owed. The potlatches were usually part of an important event such as marriage or the giving of a name. The gifts were a living symbol of the host's privileges and honors, and the giver let everyone know it:

> I am the only great tree, I the chief. I am the only great tree, I the chief. You here are right under me, tribes! You are my younger brothers under me, tribes! You surround me like a fence, tribes. I am your Eagle, the chief.

An important potlatch could take many years to arrange. First there was the process of accumulating the neccssary items to be given away. This was followed by a diplomatic period during which representatives were scnt to the various guests to work out the etiquette of the projected feast. The Quinault of Washington paid members of their own family to prepare the necessary food and paid other kinsmen to keep an account of what gifts the different guests should get and in what order they should be called on. The event itself had all the pageantry of a royal banquet. Guests were concerned about where they sat and in what order they were called to get their gifts, as well as in the quality and quantity of their gifts. *Everything* had to be eaten before the feast ended. When there was only one blanket left, the proud host placed it over his arm and asked, "Who will take it?" The guest who responded was taking responsibility for staging the next potlatch.

A rich man could rarely afford to give more than a few full-scale potlatches during his entire lifetime. The immediate effect of the event was to bankrupt him, although in time he would regain everything with interest at other potlatches where he was a guest. After the coming of the whites, the potlatches were increasingly influenced by their practices such as gifts having to be paid with interest. The decrease in Indian population because of disease also meant hereditary wealth accumulated on fewer individuals. The increasingly spectacular potlatches became wasteful exercises in ego with property and even human life destroyed to display wealth and power. These later potlatches with their accompanying abusive language have obscured the origins of the custom. The Kwakiutl of Vancouver Island speak of potlatches as wars of property rather than wars of blood. Fighting with goods and words seemed a vast improvement over spears and arrows. If two individuals were in competition for a bride or a title, they might stage rivalry potlatches rather than going to war. One Kwakiutl commented, "Now we fight with buttons, blankets, and other kinds of property. Oh, how good is the new time." The potlatchers also had play potlatches in which people laughed over the excessive language and imaginary gifts. Certainly the original potlatch custom had some of this feeling as well. The potlatches and gift giving also served to reward desired behavior patterns, especially among the young.

During the height of the potlatch fever, many minor gift-giving occasions were demanded of men of wealth. Again this is similar to the modern capitalist who must give generous tips to retain his popularity. A potlatcher had influence only so long as he had wealth he was willing to give away. His own artistic skills and knowledge were unimportant as long as he had the means to hire specialists. His gifts were a mixture of salaries, tips, loans, and bribes. An important man was also obliged to make up for social mishaps and disgraces with face-saving gifts or potlatches. So these fishing societies concentrated on the ability to gain riches. A successful person was thrifty and industrious. Marriages were planned as if they were business transactions. The man looked to increase his privileges and a woman sought a man who was as prestigious as possible as her worth was realized through his potlatches. Very much like the hardworking Puritans of New England, the potlatch people were taught to eat moderately and to work hard.

Wealth came in many forms. Dried fish, fine furs, and fish oil were basic, as were created objects such as canoes, blankets, baskets, and jewelry. The potlatchers had no money as such, but they used blankets, dentalia, and copper plaques as substitutes. Blankets were accumulated by the thousands and were handed out as small change. Dentalia were special conical sea shells fished up by the Nootka and placed on strings of special lengths. Whites who

Fishermen of the northwest coast and rivers wore clothing different from most native North Americans and were among the minority of tribes to grow mustaches. (*Huntington Free Library, Heye Foundation*)

thought dentalia money found in the sea was silly were reminded by Indians that the yellow metal they prized could be found in the bottom of streams or in the earth. The Yurok of California decorated the dentalia with carvings and feathers and made it precise lengths. They were so possessed with the idea of accumulating it that their males were taught to have it constantly on their minds. Like some cartoon burlesque of a striver, they would awake at night shouting to the spirits that they wanted to be rich. They could be heard screaming aloud, "I want dentalia." The most prestigious signs of wealth, however, were copper plates of a foot to three feet in length. These were often decorated with designs, and their use meant the occasion was extremely serious. They became more and more valuable as they were traded. Originally, they had been associated with ancestor regard and were called "bones of the dead." Some coppers were given individual names and were protected from destruction as many coppers were broken in intense rivalry potlatches.

The lush forests provided yet another kind of wealth. Redwood and red cedar were easily carved. Northwest craftsmen made dugout canoes, houses, and utensils of all kinds. The canoes were carved directly from tree trunks and could be over thirty feet long. They were made without nails by simple animal tooth and stone tools, yet they could handle the roughest seas. The rectangular plank houses of the fishing societies were equally well built. They might extend for a hundred feet and often had slatted windows like modern Venetian blinds. Potlatchers also used wood to make everything from bowls to cradles and coffins.

Their most impressive artistic achievements were their totem poles and house façades. The first poles were seen by whites in 1794 and the art reached its peak in the hundred years which followed. The totem poles were not worshiped and they did not depict gods. Like most potlatcher customs, the totem building was a tribute to an owner's name. The poles told of a claim to being descended from the time of creation or to having a special relationship with the spiritual prototype of important animals. They symbolized the history of a family much as the heraldry, crests, and flags of the European medieval societies did. Fights over the merits and heights of poles became the cause of feuds. More than one killing stemmed from a villager raising a totem higher than that of his neighbor. Despite the nastiness sometimes surrounding them, the stunning totems and carved façades were sculpturing feats unrivaled in North America.

Economics tended to make the structure of potlatch societies rigid. The democracy and harmony that prevailed in most Indian societies were absent. There were nobles, commoners, and slaves. The nobles had special dances and privileges which they claimed went back "to the dawn of the world." But it was their wealth alone that gave them power. A chief's daughter would brag, "I am seated on coppers and have many names and privileges that will be given by my father to my future husband." Even cradle songs were tied to wealth. A boy child would be told, "Don't sleep, your paddle will fall into the water and your spear too. Don't sleep, for the ravens and cranes are flying away." A girl child would be told, "Don't sleep too much. Your digging stick will fall into the water and your basket. Wake up! It is nearly low water. You will be late going down to the beach."

Commoners might occasionally become rich if they were extremely industrious, talented, or lucky. Their best hope to advancement was to be in the service of a rich relative. An individual who had a striking vision or a skill in war or carving might attract the favor of a rich kinsman. Visions were critical, for without them a youth would not be taught a skill. Visionless young men often spent the night in terrifying places or scratched themselves bloody with thorns to bring on a dream. A rich youth usually dreamed of his favorite rich relative or the society he wanted to join. Commoners had ordinary visions and slaves rarely dreamed at all. A woman who

The people of the Northwest were among the world's greatest
wood sculptors. The Bella Bella made the death mask, the
Kwakiutl made the mechanical, potlatch mask, and the Tlingit
made the totem pole. (*Courtesy of Museum of the American
Indian, Heye Foundation*)

dreamed became a shaman.

Slaves had no chance to advance, for they were property and were treated as such, even being killed at some potlatches as an ultimate show of waste. Most slaves were women, and the Indian Puritans kept them healthy so that they could do all the routine and dull work. Although slaves could be bought, they were usually taken in raids. They might be stolen back or ransomed, but a face-saving potlatch was a must. Some nobles preferred to let their family members remain in captivity rather than go to the expense of a face-saving potlatch. Among the Yurok, a man could volunteer for slavery to pay off his debts, but men were usually not enslaved because they tried to escape and planned serious retaliations.

Even war was affected by the potlatch mentality. Some fights were agreed upon in advance, but most were in the form of surprise raids. The night before an attack, each warrior took omens to see how his luck was. A death warning or bad sign of any sort was sufficient grounds for a volunteer to dismiss himself with no loss of honor. The raids were often followed by peace negotiations where the potlatch rules came into their own. Neutral bargainers came from each side to go over the details of every killing, injury, and property damage with all the vigor of modern lawyers and insurance agents. Ceremonial and ritual damages were counted as equal to "real" damages. The Yurok fed their love of dentalia by making a payment necessary for every offense from trespassing to premeditated murder. Rather than an absolute value for injuries, there was a sliding scale with the penalty adjusted to the guilty one's ability to pay. This made for a lot of discussion and haggling, which the potlatchers liked. The rights of injured nobles were considered more important than those of commoners, which added yet another opportunity for establishing status.

Potlatch women were viewed as producers of wealth for their men. A noble might have many wives who worked hard themselves and who saw that their slaves were industrious in picking fruit, finding shellfish, weaving blankets, drying fish, and making baskets. Divorce was rare because of the required face-saving potlatch. During adolescence a girl must go into isolation for as long as a year in order to perform rituals and observe taboos. The rationale for this was that her suffering guaranteed future riches. Young women were constantly chaperoned and were expected to remain virgins. A lullaby from the northern tribes painted a rather glum picture for why women were born at all:

In order to insure a good salmon catch, ceremonies like this one were performed by the coastal people. (*Huntington Free Library, Heye Foundation*)

The little girl will pick wild roses.
That is why she was born.

The little girl will dig wild rice with her fingers.
That is why she was born.

She will gather sap of pitch pine trees in the spring.
She will pick strawberries and blueberries.
That is why she was born.

She will pick soapberries and elderberries.
She will pick wild roses.
That is why she was born.

When the Europeans began to sail into the area in the 1740s, the potlatchers entered a new era of wealth. Hundreds of ships called between 1774 and 1800. Their crews included many Chinese, Hawaiians, and Filipinos, who taught the Indians new carving skills. Many new products such as nails made life much easier. The whites took otter furs and other skins which they used to trade for the valuables of the Far East. The Indians called the beautiful Yankee clipper ships "Bostons" and their British counterparts were "King Georges." The greed of the potlatchers now fed on the goods the ships brought. Totem poles found new heights. Carvings were more skillful. Brass replaced stone. Guns and steel traps replaced harpoons, bows, and spears. The most profound change came with the establishment of the Hudson's Bay Company trading post in a place near present-day Seattle.

The gray blankets of the Hudson's Bay Company became so common they were a new currency. Few Indians bothered now with weaving blankets from animal skin or hair. Even fewer clung to the established patterns of animal conservation their fathers had taught them. The whites wanted furs and the whites were willing to pay well for them. The Indians felt released from traditional beliefs. Under the protection of the white man's magic, they hunted for hundreds of miles around the fort. They soon wiped out all the game just as the whites would one day wipe away almost all the salmon. They discarded the wisdom accumulated by their nations over the ages. In their frantic rush for wealth, they committed suicide.

Formal potlatches reached absurd proportions because there were far too many goods to be useful. Potlatches became more frequent and were grand displays of waste. Families were living extravagantly just to impress their neighbors. Populations dwindled as the white diseases struck. People like the Chinook disappeared entirely. Noble families died out. Commoners joined the crew of a ship and returned with more money than the most prosperous chiefs of old.

The system crashed into oblivion with the opening of the Oregon Trail in 1842. Within ten years, Oregon and Washington would be territories of the United States, California would have a Gold Rush, and the potlatchers would learn about reservations. Some tribes fought militarily but the groups were too small and scattered. Most of them found it easier to adapt to the new system and were more at ease within it than any previous Indian people had been. The transition was not without pain, however, and a Nootka song about the perpetual rain clouds could be given a new interpretation:

> *Don't you ever,*
> *you up in the sky,*
> *don't you ever get tired*
> *of having clouds between you and us?*

The potlatchers were a strange people with many disagreeable characteristics, but they were Indians and they placed importance on spiritual values. They had great respect for the dead and put much faith in shamans and the salmon spirits. Women were often shamans, and in some tribes only women could be shamans. The most impressive religious rituals took place in the forest. The Indians believed that in the beginning, creation had been put into order by a power related to one of the more clever creatures such as Raven or Mink. Dramatic dancing and feasting retold the creation myth as the Indians used grotesque masked figures to inspire and frighten one another. During these ceremonies, shamans might be possessed and be taken in a dream to Wolf or Salmon Village, where the spirits taught them arts to aid their people. The villagers danced to honor animal spirits, and the campfires often cast strange forest shadows as the skillful masked dancers acted out the exploits of Wolf or Cannibal Monster. Within their own value systems, the Northwesterners created a theater/religious event on the same artistic level as the more widely known efforts of the Pueblo.

Much has been written about the unpleasant, vain, and materialistic nature of the fishing people, especially in comparison to the gentle Pueblo. It is almost as if the whites were shocked to see their own values apparently mocked in such a stark fashion. But the potlatchers were very much concerned with traditional Indian spiritual values. Chief Seattle of the Suquamish and Duwamish addressed a warning to the whites of the state of Washington in 1855 which is one of the most eloquent of all Indian speeches:

> Your religion was written upon tables of stone by the iron finger of your God so that you could not forget. The Red Man could never comprehend nor

remember it. Our religion is the traditions of our ancestors—the dreams of our old men, given to them in the solemn hours of night by the Great Spirit; and the visions of our sachems and is written in the hearts of our people.

Your dead cease to love you and the land of their nativity as soon as they pass the portals of the tomb and wander way beyond the stars. Our dead never forget the beautiful world that gave them being . . .

A few more moons. A few more winters—and not one of the descendants of the mighty hosts that once moved over this broad land or lived in happy homes, protected by the Great Spirit, will remain to mourn over the graves of a people—once more powerful and hopeful than yours. But why should I mourn at the untimely fate of my people? Tribe follows tribe, and nation follows nation, like the waves of the sea. It is the order of nature, and to regret it is useless. Your time of decay may be distant, but it will surely come, for even the White Man whose God walked and talked with him as friend with friend cannot be exempt from the common destiny. We may be brothers after all. We will see.

. . . Every part of this soil is sacred in the estimation of my people. Every hillside, every valley, every plain and grove has been hallowed by some sad or happy event in days long vanished. Even the rocks, which seem to be dumb and dead as they swelter in the sun along the silent shore, thrill with memories of stirring events connected with the lives of my people, and the very dust upon which you now stand responds more lovingly to their footsteps than to yours, because it is rich with the blood of our ancestors and our bare feet are conscious of the sympathetic touch . . . And when the last Red Man shall have perished, and the memory of my tribe shall have become a myth among the White

Men, these shores will swarm with the invisible dead of my tribe, and when your children's children think themselves alone in the field, the store, the shop, upon the highway, or in the silence of the pathless woods, they will not be alone. In all the earth there is no place dedicated to solitude. At night when the streets of your cities and villages are silent and you think them deserted, they will throng with the returning hosts that once filled and still love this beautiful land. The White Man will never be alone.

Let him be just and deal kindly with my people, for the dead are not powerless. Dead, did I say? There is no death, only a change of worlds.

THE LONGEST MARCH

All the people of the plateau made the journey from good will to hatred for the whites, but the Nez Percé rode the saddest trail of all. They lived east of the potlatchers in the valleys of the Clearwater, the Salmon, and the Snake rivers. In this region where Washington, Oregon, and Idaho meet there were deep canyons, ridges, and evergreen forests. The valleys ranged in width from virtually nothing as in the case of famous Hell's Canyon to narrow bottomlands from one half to three fourths of a mile wide. Beyond the canyons were hills and occasional flat or rolling prairies. The seasons were clearly defined. Summer meant grasses and flowering prairies, while winter brought biting frost and deep snows. The Nez Percé land was not well suited to the interests of the whites but the tall regal people prized their valleys above all things known beneath the sky.

Salmon was the main food of the Nez Percé and permanent settlements existed near the best streams which were recognized as the territory of specific bands, but deer, bear, and mountain sheep provided variety in Nez Percé diets. The American horse had become extinct in prehistoric times, but the Europeans had brought horses with them, and the Nez Percé loved the new animal very much. They became among the most skillful tribes not only in handling horses but in breeding and trading them. Horses allowed the Nez Percé to travel and hunt much easier than before. They began to use the western edge of the plains for buffalo hunting and adopted many of the habits of the people of the plains. The other salmon-eating Indians called the Nez Percé "horse Indians" to mark them off from the salmon eaters on the coast who traveled mainly on foot or by canoe.

Lewis and Clark entered the Nez Percé and Shoshone country in 1806 as part of their exploration of the Louisana Purchase. The explorers had a young Shoshone woman with them whose reunion with her tribe created immense good will for the Americans, but such good will was only an extension of the usual hospitality for strangers. The Nez Percé were always noted for treating traders and visitors with kindness. The white men who came up the great rivers wanted to trade their products for the things of the forest, an arrangement which left Indian life pretty much as the whites had found it. A new prosperity swept the region but the awful price was the killing diseases of the whites that came up the same rivers as the trading canoes. Along the main routes of trade, people such as the Chinook, who had always been among the most eager to barter, became extinct. The scourge of 1831 was smallpox, but each year a new disease came to take heavy tolls, with cholera which killed thousands in 1849 being among the worst. The Nez

Percé were alarmed by this march of death and when they heard of a Holy Book whose magic was mightier than anything else the whites possessed they were anxious to have its protection. In 1831 they sent a delegation one thousand miles to speak with their friend Clark who was living in St. Louis. The explorer was sympathetic toward their desire for the new religion, but he said he could not agree to sending missionaries when the new trail was still so dangerous. Only one of the Nez Percé travelers survived the return trip. He told his people that Rabbitskin Leggings, the leader of the delegation, had told Clark: "I came with one eye partly opened. I sought light. I return with both eyes shut and my arms broken."

In less than ten years the formidable thousand miles of dangerous trail became a crowded roadway bringing not one set of reluctant missionaries but many competing groups. Marcus Whitman was the first to establish a permanent white settlement. He opened the Oregon Trail in 1841–42 and welcomed a thousand travelers the next year. The new whites were not loners who came by mule or canoe but entire families loaded with housewares, tools, children, and livestock. Their heavy prairie schooners cut deep ruts into the soil as they took weeks to cross the rivers of the West before resting in safety at Fort Hill. Eventually they pushed on to Fort Boise and from there to the Columbia River, which took them to the fertile territories of Washington and Oregon. By 1852, the settlers were passing through at the rate of ten thousand a year.

These first waves of immigration did not disturb the Nez Percé. The travelers were too anxious to reach the valleys beyond the mountains to consider stopping in the difficult country with the harsh winters. Many tribes were so unconcerned about the whites that they actually helped them cross dangerous rivers and collected stray cattle for

them. Some joked about the pale faces of the strangers, but
many of them never saw a white at all. Yellow Wolf of the
Nez Percé would remember these days with fondness. He
spoke of the mountains, springs and running waters "of
my own country when only Indians were there. Of tepees
along the bending river. Of the blue clear lake, wide mead-
ows with horse and cattle herds. From the mountain forests,
voices seemed to be calling. I felt as dreaming."

The tribes of Washington and Oregon had different at-
titudes. The valleys the whites desired were their home-
lands. Wars broke out with increasing fury and frequency.
The Indians fought so well that most of the settlements
were closed down, but the victory was only momentary.
Soon, fresh waves of immigrants with new types of rifles
came down the Columbia. Tribes such as the Spokane
and Coeur d'Alene which had never fought before took up
arms. The Nez Percé were urged to join the struggle, but
they refused. They even protected whites when the Marcus
Whitman Mission fell to the Cayuse, who had always been
friends and neighbors. The Nez Percé thought of themselves as peaceful and reasonable folk. They could not
imagine why there should ever be war between them and
the United States.

Some of the Nez Percé adopted the Christian religion or
wove parts of it into their traditional faiths, but a large
number remained loyal to the Dreamer Cult, which stressed
the sacred nature of the earth. Chief Joseph the Younger
explained some of the cult's basic beliefs to a white commission:

> [The Creative Power] was made of the earth and
> grew up on her bosom. The earth was his mother
> and nurse and was sacred to his affection . . . More-
> over the earth carried chieftainship . . . and there-

fore to part with the earth would be to part with himself or his self-control.

Toohulhulsote, one of the chief advocates of the Dreamer Cult, said, "The earth is part of my body." Such attachment to the land led the Nez Percé to be careful about making any treaties, but the Dreamer faith went beyond generalized nature worship to instill moral virtues. Chief Joseph the Younger explained that the Nez Percé were taught that they should never be the first to break a bargain, that it was a disgrace to tell a lie, and that a great spirit saw and heard everything on earth. Early settlers remarked that when Nez Percé were witnesses at trials they refused to hold up their hand and take an oath because they spoke the truth all the time.

These truthtellers so attached to the earth called themselves Nimpau—the real people. The name Nez Percé most likely stemmed from a time in their past when they had worn ornaments in their noses, a practice they had given up by the time of Lewis and Clark. The tribe was always noted for its passive nature but as the 1850s wore on, the whites demanded treaties. In 1855 the head men reluctantly agreed to give up some land with the guarantee that all the remaining valleys would remain Indian for "as long as the grass shall grow and the water flow." The matter seemed settled until 1861 when gold was discovered on Nez Percé land. A new agreement was negotiated, temporarily opening additional lands for mining. Two years later the whites demanded more land and the chiefs, who had been hesitant before, refused to sign away any more territory. The councils of the Nez Percé met and the tribe divided into three equal factions.

The group that would come to be called the Treaty Nez Percé agreed to sign the new treaty because the land to be given up was not part of their territory even though they would share in the gifts which came with the agreement. A second group absolutely refused to consider giving up any more land. The third block regretted having signed any treaties and demanded that the lands already given up be returned. Among the nonsigners were Looking Glass the Elder and Joseph the Elder. These head men had been wary about signing in the first place for they understood that he who has the right to give also has the right to take away. The whites had no valid claim to their land. Joseph believed that no man owned any part of the earth and thus no man could sell any part of it. The signatures of the Treaty Nez Percé could no more bind the entire nation than one third of the Senate could bind the United States. But the Indian Bureau had long made it official policy to accept such convenient absurdities as justice. Those who would not go on reservations they had never agreed to go on and would not give up land they had never agreed to give up were termed "hostiles." Only the shock of the Civil War and the remoteness of the Nez Percé region allowed the dispute to remain unsettled. Old Joseph was so disgusted with the whites he tore up a Bible he had possessed for thirty years and vowed he would no longer have anything to do with the whites.

Not a summer passed from that time on when an army agent or a spokesman for the Indian Bureau did not attempt to persuade the Non-Treaties to accept reservations. At the close of the Civil War more whites moved west and they began to settle in the plateau region in greater numbers than before. The Nez Percé prepared summaries of their positions and sent them to Washington, D.C. President Grant was so impressed by the merits of their arguments that in 1873 he signed an executive order returning half the land the Non-Treaties had never signed away. Idaho whites became so enraged over the President's decision that their political representatives were able to get it reversed in less than two years. The chiefs who had refused to sign died but in their places were Looking Glass the Younger and Joseph the Younger, two shrewd and able leaders whose abilities matched their patriotism.

The fatal hour for the Non-Treaties struck in 1877. The Modoc to the south had fought their incredible war only a few years before and the Sioux to the east had annihilated Custer the previous summer but the United States still thought it could handle the Nez Percé roughly. The tribe had never fought whites. They were famous for their good sense and co-operation. The orders went out that they must go to a reservation immediately or the army would arrest them. General Howard made the ultimatum unnecessarily cruel by posting a thirty-day limit for the surrender. The herds and villages of the Non-Treaties were widely scattered. If they were to reach the designated spot on a nearby prairie by the deadline of June 15, they had to cross the formidable Snake and Grand Ronde rivers. Howard would find crossing the rough waters a terrible ordeal for his own tough soldiers just a few weeks later but at this point he expected families to transport all their possessions and numerous animals over the rivers in a relatively short space of time.

Both Joseph and Looking Glass had chosen to comply. The Nez Percé head men were not foolish. They realized they could not win an armed struggle with the United States. General Howard's ultimatum might well have succeeded except for some of the younger warriors. The Nez Percé had been peaceful Indians but as always in relations between Indians and whites there were a number of unpunished murders on both sides which made violence possible at any time. Earlier, Howard had imprisoned Toohulhulsote for insolence and for insisting on the traditional Nez Percé customs. Now the army wanted to take all the Non-Treaty land. The white chief was making the tribes lose valuable livestock by forcing them to cross treacherous rivers at a difficult time of the year. If the Nez Percé head men were old women who feared death, there were at least three young braves who would defend the honor of the nation, avenge the dead, and protect the beliefs of the Dreamers. The self-styled heroes put on their war paint and began a series of raids which resulted in a dozen dead whites.

The news of the killings came to Joseph's band while it was still trying to comply with Howard's demands. The chief understood at once that the army might not be overly careful about locating exactly which braves in which band had committed the murders. Joseph decided to move his people to White Bird Canyon to await developments. Within a short time, other groups of Non-Treaties began to join him. The chiefs did not approve of what their young warriors had done but they would not give them up to the inconsistencies of white justice. Many killers of their own people had gone unpunished.

Looking Glass had not joined the outbreak. He sent word to his neighbors not to go near his lodges and involve his group in their "useless and foolish struggle." Joseph and the other men debated on the possibility of making some sort of bargain with the angry whites, but a force of one hundred army volunteers cut short their council. The whites imagined they could score an easy victory as the Nez Percé had no reputation as fighting men. These volunteers became the first to discover that the Nez Percé were the finest marksmen of all the Indians with an un-usually good sense of tactics. A handful of Nez Percé ap-proached the whites under a truce flag but they were immediately fired upon and forced to take cover to save their lives. The whites charged valiantly but within a short time a third of them were dead and the seventy warriors who had dropped them were chasing the survivors across the canyon floor.

The Nez Percé were elated with their easy triumph, but they were divided over future tactics. The various points of view discussed at the White Bird councils would be repeated throughout the course of the war which followed. Joseph wanted to stay in the valley and fight. Either the whites would be persuaded to let them have a reservation in their old territories or the Nez Percé would perish defending their one true homeland. Others argued that they should move to the land of the Crow which was out of General Howard's department. The whites in other regions would have no reason to persecute them. Still others thought it best to unite with the Sioux in an intertribal confederation for survival. The Nez Percé had never fought against whites before but they had already won the first battle of a running war that would carry them through more than one thousand miles of enemy soldiers, cultivated valleys, and wildernesses. They would win any number of skirmishes with the military yet retain enough discipline to spare civilian populations. The talking wires would carry news of their heroic struggle to the entire United States and perhaps for the first time in North American history there would be many whites who wished Indians some sort of victory.

Upon hearing of the White Bird Canyon debacle General Howard ordered his troops to march against the Nez Percé. He foolishly complicated his task by sending a detachment to round up the band of Looking Glass. Making no effort to determine the mood of the band, the troops attacked the unguarded camp as if it were the center of Nez

Percé resistance. The toll in families and warriors was high but the majority of the band fled to safety. When the angered tribesmen regathered they decided to join the hostiles rather than submit to such brutal intimidation. Looking Glass became one of the major war leaders of the united hostiles, and his braves would seek revenge for their slain relatives in many future battles. While Howard's detachment was busy creating such substantial new enemies, his main body of three hundred men accomplished nothing. The hostiles had left White Bird Canyon and thrown Howard off their trail by crossing and recrossing the Salmon River. On July 3 an army scouting party of ten was wiped out by Nez Percé ambushers. The army began its painful re-evaluation of Nez Percé bravery and military ability.

The Non-Treaties made their new camp on the Clearwater River and thereby committed their first and only major error of the campaign. If they were to achieve success against the army they needed to remain mobile but at Clearwater the bands set up a semipermanent camp. They had the foresight to build defensive rifle pits, a device which characterized all future camps, but other than that the Indians made no preparations to defend themselves. Their strength had grown to two hundred warriors and four hundred women, children, and aged.

The Nez Percé scouts had spotted every previous army move but on July 11, Howard surprised the camp. His force was made up of four hundred regulars, two hundred volunteers, and assorted units of artillery. Even with surprise added to his overwhelming numerical advantage, he was not able to overrun the Nez Percé positions. The rifle pits with their rock protection were well placed and precise marksmanship drove the attackers back. The following day a fresh assault found the camp deserted. The casualties in the battle were few. Howard lost thirteen killed and twenty-seven wounded. He estimated that the Nez Percé lost twice as many although the Indians would only admit four killed and six wounded when questioned after the war. The significance of the battle was not in the loss of life but in the destruction or capture of almost all of the considerable possessions of the Nez Percé. Joseph would write that Howard broke him upon the Clearwater, and white historians refer to the battle as the Gettysburg of the Nez Percé. The nation had been wealthy and it was a hard blow to lose everything in a single battle, but the Nez Percé still retained their fighting ability and determination to resist. Joseph was willing to fight a battle to the death in the valleys but the council decided it was best that the tribe move to buffalo country.

Howard pursued the fleeing Nez Percé to the banks of the Klamath River where his force was held off by a rear guard of Nez Percé fighting men. The Indians now struck out across the treacherous Lolo Trail that led over the Bitterroot Mountains. Howard found it impossible to move with any speed along the route and telegraphed ahead for others to delay the Indians while he tried to catch up. At a gap in the mountains a barricade was hastily constructed by thirty soldiers and three hundred civilians. When the Nez Percé arrived at the barrier they told the civilians that their fight was not with them but with General Howard. They did not want to kill any whites and they certainly had no quarrel with the people of the Bitterroot Valley. If they were allowed free passage through the area they promised they would neither loot nor kill. The settlers knew the reputation of the Nez Percé and the Indian diplomats were so eloquent that the tribe was allowed to pass by the barricade that came to be remembered as Fort Fizzle. At towns in the valley the Indians made purchases of sugar, coffee, tobacco, and other goods with their remaining gold dust and greenbacks. Not all the young men could be restrained but the chiefs kept their word as much as possible. Their train sometimes stretched for as long as three miles and contained two to three thousand horses. The slight damage suffered by the people of Bitterroot was nothing compared to the deaths a battle at the gap would have entailed.

The Indians did not camp again until they reached a valley beyond the Continental Divide. They thought they would have time to rest and enjoy themselves, but they were mistaken. Colonel Gibbon had left Fort Shaw with orders to find them. He pushed his men day and night, and when scouts brought word of the Nez Percé camp, he rushed to attack. During the first moments of the charge, it seemed the Indians were about to suffer a defeat surpassing the one upon the Clearwater. White Bird and Looking Glass happened to be isolated at opposite ends of the camp by the attack. Soon their strong voices rallied the stunned Nez Percé warriors. The Indian rout suddenly turned into its opposite. Gibbon's men fell back in panic shouting that they had been trapped in the same manner Custer had been trapped. The Indian counterattack was so sweeping that the warriors even captured Gibbon's cannon. If the Nez Percé had known how to use artillery, Gibbon's men would have been pounded to death by their own guns. Joseph's role in the actual fighting was slight as he had the responsibility of gathering up the supplies and leading the nonfighters to safety.

Gibbon gathered his men on high ground where Nez Percé rifle fire immobilized them. The main body of Indians returned to their camp to find that of the eighty-seven dead, seventy were women, children, and the old. Gibbon would write:

Few of us will soon forget the wail of mingled rage and horror which came from the camp four or five hundred yards from us when the Indians returned to it and recognized their slaughtered warriors, women, and children. Above this wail of horror we could hear the passionate appeal of the leaders urging their followers to fight and the war hoops in answer which boded us no good.

The warriors buried their dead and gradually filtered back to the rifle pits and again their deadly accuracy terrified the whites. The sharpshooters would undoubtedly have shot and starved Gibbon's men to death but word reached them that the plodding General Howard was approaching. The Nez Percé retreated, leaving the army with thirty-three dead and thirty-eight wounded. Howard was shocked when he came upon the destroyed Gibbon, as he had thought the Clearwater battle had meant the war was finished. His Bannock scouts had been promised horses. Their anger drove them to dig up the corpses of the dead Nez Percé to mutilate and scalp them. When the Nez Percé heard of this outrage they were horrified and their estimation of Howard's character diminished.

The new trails of the Nez Percé led them through Yellowstone National Park, which was just five years old. The Indians moved efficiently and quickly but many individuals took the opportunity to gaze at the spurting geysers of steam and the bubbling mudpits. The head men strove to control their young warriors, but several touring parties were harassed and two whites lost their lives. By a quirk of fate General Sherman, the chief of all the armies of the white nation, was visiting in the park. Sherman no more suspected the presence of the Nez Percé than they suspected his. The tribesmen would have been able to capture him easily had they been aware he was so near.

The tribe maneuvered cleverly. Their false trails and decoy herds were so effective that several sizable groups sent against them were thrown off the trail completely or hopelessly delayed. Looking Glass, White Bird, Toohulhulsote, Lean Elk, and Poker Joe were among the influential Nez Percé leaders. The success of the tribe was a group effort but the white newspapers spoke only of Joseph who was given sole credit for outwitting so many white adversaries.

The Indians came out of the park at Clark's Fork on the Yellowstone River. They met some Crow who were willing to give them supplies but could not harbor Non-Treaties because they were army scouts and had good relations with the whites. At this point the only alternative left to the Nez Percé was to cross to Canada and join Sitting Bull. Even though the Crow refused to scout against the Nez Percé, Major General Sturgis, commander of the reorganized 7th Regiment, learned about their location. Vigorous marches enabled the regiment to catch the Indians at their camp at Canyon Creek in Montana. The white pony soldiers were fatigued from their march, yet the Indians who had been on the march so much longer threw back their initial attacks easily. Not even a spirited charge by Custer's old regiment seeking desperately to restore its lost prestige could shake the Nez Percé defense. The Indians began to withdraw under the cover of darkness, and the weary cavalrymen had neither the will nor the resources to give pursuit.

What proved to be the last Nez Percé camp was pitched forty miles south of the Canadian border in the Bear Paw Mountains. The tribe had never fought whites until their homeland was demanded. Even in war they had shown an extraordinary discipline and honor that the various civilian and military units sent against them rarely equaled. They had maneuvered and fought as well as any tribe and they had overcome artillery, the talking wire, and continual fresh troops. They were willing to leave the United States forever, but the army would not allow them even that last comfort. Colonel Miles with Cheyenne scouts and six hundred fresh men steamed and marched 150 miles to attack them during the last days of September. He brought machine guns and cannon. Much of the camp was already packed for the final dash into exile when he struck.

Miles ordered a full mounted charge on the camp, thinking to smash resistance with one decisive blow. The Nez Percé had marched so far and suffered so many wounds, Miles assumed the warriors would snap. Such was not the case. The accurate Nez Percé rifle fire brought down 20 per cent of the advancing soldiers. Even if the charge had managed to capture the rifle pits, the casualty rate would have been considered high. As it was, the charge was a failure. Miles had to call retreat. A little over one hundred weary warriors had turned back one of the best trained cavalry units. Miles consoled himself with the thought that at least he had the Nez Percé trapped, but he soon wondered about that, too, as Nez Percé sharpshooters selected his officers as special targets. Snow began to fall. Miles was no longer certain whether he was besieger or the besieged.

The men under Miles fought back with courage equal to that of the Indians. The Nez Percé lost seventeen dead and more than forty wounded. Toohulhulsote, Poker Joe, Looking Glass, and other leaders were killed. The deaths of so many important men were disheartening, but the only two chiefs of major status left alive, Joseph and White Bird, would not surrender. They sent runners to Sitting Bull to ask his assistance.

The Nez Percé messengers never reached the Sioux medicine man. The Indians assumed that some Assiniboin killed them out of fear of being drawn into a new war with the whites. Other sources brought the news of the battle, and the Sioux wanted to ride to the rescue at once. The Canadian Northwest Mounted Police rode into camp to warn the Sioux that if they should recross the border to fight they would lose all rights of political asylum and sanctuary. While Sitting Bull's council meditated, Miles was suffering badly. In one group of 115 men, he had lost 53 killed or wounded. In other companies he had lost one third of his men with 40 more wounded. There were almost no facilities for tending the injured and the weather grew progressively worse. It was with relief that Miles discovered Joseph wanted to discuss possible peace terms. The chief came under a flag of truce and a reporter assigned to the army got his first glimpse of the Indian whose exploits had thrilled the whites of the United States:

> Physically Joseph is a splendid-looking man. He is fully six feet high; in the prime of life—about 35, has a splendid face and well-formed head. His forehead is high, his eyes bright yet kind, his nose finely cut, and his mouth though determined, rather too sad-looking for actual beauty.

Joseph was inclined to surrender but even with most of the other leaders dead he was still not in complete control of the Indian camp. Unable to reach a satisfactory agreement the chief was about to return to his own people when Miles had him seized. The colonel was frustrated by the faltering siege and the prospect that the thousand-mile campaign might yet end in failure. His treachery was not premeditated like the treachery of General Jesup with the Seminole chief Osceola but, though many thousands of miles and many thousands of days separated the cold of Montana from the sunshine of Florida, a white general again forsook his honor to arrest an Indian carrying a white truce flag. Joseph escaped the fate of his Seminole counterpart only because his own men happened to capture a white officer. An ashamed Miles was forced to trade his valuable "prisoner" for one of his subordinates.

On October 4 General Howard arrived to reinforce Miles. He had patiently stayed on the trail of the Nez Percé the entire distance from Idaho. The military situation was now hopeless for the Non-Treaties. Joseph was disturbed about the welfare of his people. Many of them were wandering helplessly in the mountains with little food and scant protection from the cold. His men were weak. There had been no word from Sitting Bull. The decision to go to Canada had been forced on them. The Nez Percé did not object to reservation life so much if they could have land in one of their old valleys. He had counseled peace at many meetings and now he offered to surrender if the whites would respect certain terms: his people must be cared for in Montana until spring when they could be returned to a reservation in the valleys of Idaho. After a brief consideration of Joseph's proposal, Miles and Howard agreed. Joseph responded with a surrender message that brought tears to the eyes of the Nez Percé interpreters and moved even the hardened military men by its stoic eloquence:

> Tell General Howard I know his heart. What he told me before I have in my heart. I am tired of fighting. Looking Glass is dead. Toohulhulsote is dead. The old men are all dead. It is the young who say yes or no. He who led on the young is dead. It is cold and we have no blankets. The little children are freezing to death. My people, some of them, have run away to the hills, and have no blankets, no food. No one knows where they

are, perhaps freezing to death. I want to have time to look for my children and see how many of them I can find. Maybe I shall find them among the dead. Hear me my chiefs, I am tired; my heart is sick and sad. From where the sun now stands I will fight no more forever.

The army men were astounded by the weak condition of the surrendering warriors. The formidable enemy who had eluded them over so many miles consisted mainly of hardy women and children protected by a few incredibly brave men. Howard had understood from the start that he was pursuing a band of families and not a war party but only in the moments of final surrender did he realize the problems the Indian chiefs had faced.

White Bird was so skeptical of white honor that he slipped away with his followers to the camp of Sitting Bull. The old chief spoke often of Captain Jack and thought that since the killers who started the outbreak were from his group he might be held responsible for their actions. He also doubted the whites would keep their pledge regarding a reservation in Idaho. Events proved White Bird correct.

The Nez Percé who surrendered were first taken to Bismarck, North Dakota, where the townspeople behaved as no white people had ever before behaved toward captured Indians. They presented the tribe with food and much needed clothing. They made no secret of their best wishes for the defeated Nez Percé. Such behavior proved to be the last translation of favorable public opinion into positive acts that the Nez Percé would experience. Miles wanted to keep his pledge but his superiors asserted that the peace terms were improper. The tribe was not taken to Montana but south to a military reservation at Fort Leavenworth, Kansas. Some time later the group was taken to a reservation in Oklahoma. In three agonizing years almost two hundred Nez Percé died and the rest were broken in health and spirit.

General Miles was appointed commander of the region containing Idaho in 1881. He wanted to honor his pledge to Joseph and wrote a letter to the President of the United States personally vouching for the Nez Percé character and documenting the cruelty of the Oklahoma confinement. Miles had married the daughter of a prominent senator and he was the in-law of General Sherman as well as being a famous Indian fighter in his own right. The President listened respectfully, but the residents of Idaho argued vigorously against the return of the "wild" Nez Percé. The Great White Father could not find the courage to risk political disfavor for the mere sake of justice or honoring a field agreement made by one of his most respected chiefs. He soothed his conscience by allowing the Nez Percé to be moved to Lapwai, a northern reservation. Almost at once the Presbyterian Mission there objected to having any Dreamers come to them. The Indian interpreters sent to speak with the Nez Percé asked, "Where do you want to go? Lapwai and be a Christian or Colville and just be yourself?" Joseph and most of his followers chose the Colville Reservation of the Spokane.

In the discussion which continued about the surrender, Joseph insisted he would have chosen death before giving up if Miles and Howard had not promised to return them to their homeland. The newspapers had depicted him as a red Napoleon, but he was simply a powerful voice in the councils of a people who tolerated no emperors. Even his personal fame and prestige were of no use in securing a reservation in the Wallowa Valley. People were impressed by his writings and speeches. They felt the emotion behind his simple statement, "I love that land more than all the rest of the world." But the government would not grant his one wish. It was not until 1900 that he was even allowed to visit his former home. The inspector who was required to go with him reported that the old warrior wept when he saw that a settler had taken care of his father's grave.

His own death came four summers later while he was sitting in contemplation before a fire. The agents at Colville listed "a broken heart" as the official cause of death. A former aide of General Howard would write, "I think in

This Nez Percé couple, with their dog pulling a travois, might have been one of the families that followed Joseph on the long march from Idaho to North Dakota, only to end eventually on an Oklahoma reservation. (*Courtesy of Museum of the American Indian, Heye Foundation*)

all his long career, Joseph cannot accuse the government of the United States of a single act of justice." Certainly the fate of the Native Americans was clear to Joseph as he sat before the dying flame those last years. Soon Indians would be curiosities and amusements for the whites. They would be servants or beggars or worst of all, as Black Hawk of the Wisconsin Sauk had predicted, they would be just like the whites. The Nez Percé nation was dead even though Nez Percé bodies lingered. Perhaps one day the flesh of the Indian would perish altogether leaving only his soul to cast a red shadow in the dusk. Yet when his fire snapped loudly or unexpectedly flared brightly, Joseph would remember the teachings of his people. For a short time the man the Nez Percé knew as Hein-mot Too-ya-La-kekt could dream again:

> *You ask me to plow the ground.*
> *Shall I take a knife and tear my mother's breast?*
> *Then when I die*
> *She will not take me to her bosom to sleep.*
>
> *You ask me to dig for stone.*
> *Shall I dig under her skin for bones?*
> *Then when I die*
> *I cannot enter her body to be born again.*
>
> *You ask me to cut grass and make hay,*
> *And sell it and be rich like the white man.*
> *But how dare I cut off my mother's hair?*
>
> *It is a bad law and my people cannot obey it!*

INDEX

NOTE: *Page numbers in boldface refer to illustrations.*

Acoma, sky city, 22
Agriculture, 16, 17, 28, 29, 39
Alaska, 27
Animal spirits, 18, 99
Apache Indians, **12,** 16–17, 20, 21, 27, 29, 37–52
Arizona, 15, 16, 19
Army of the West, 30
Art, 62
Assiniboin Indians, 115

Bannock Indians, 113
Bear Paw Mountains, 114
Bella Bella Indians, death masks, **94**
Berkeley Museum, 79
Betzinez, Jason (Geronimo's cousin), 38, 40, 52
Bitterroot Valley, 111, 112
Blankets, 35, 89, 90, 97
Black Hawk, Sauk Indian, 121
Bostons, clipper ships, 97
Bounties, 33
Buffalo, 87, 102

California, 16, 98
California Indians, 57–63, **81.** See also Modoc War; Yahi Indians

Camouflage, 37
Camp Grant massacre, 44, 47
Canada, 27
Canadian Northwest Mounted Police, 116
Canby, Edward Richard Sprigg, 67, 68
Canoes, 92
Canyon Creek, 114
Captain Jack, 64–72, 118
   photograph, 71
   quoted, 66
Carson, Christopher (Kit), **32,** 33
Carving, 92, 97
Catholic Church, 26, 30, 61
Cattle, 20, 47
Cayuse Indians, 104
Cherokee Indians, 33, 50–51
Children, 39, 59
Chinese, 97
Chinook Indians, 98, 102
Chiricahua Apaches, 17, 40, 42–43, 44, 50, 51
Chumash Indians, 62–63
Civil War, 32, 33, 42, 106
Clark, William, 103
Clearwater River, 101

Nez Percé battle, 110, 111, 112, 113
Cliff dwellings, 22
Clipper ships, 97
Clothing
  Apache girl, **12**
  Northwestern fishermen, **91**
Clowns, 24
Cochise, Chiricahua chief, 40–44, 46, 47
  quoted, 41
Coeur d'Alene Indians, 104
Colorado River, 16, 59
Columbia River, 103, 104
Columbus, Christopher, 17
Colville Reservation, 119, 120
Comanche Indians, 16, 29
Commoners, 93, 96, 98
Copper plaques, 90, 92
Corn, 17, 18, 19–20, 23
Coronado, Juan Vásquez de, 20
Creation myths
  Apache, 38
  California Indians, 58
  potlatchers, 99
  Pueblo, 22
  Yuma, 59
Cremation, 59
Crook, George, 44–45, 46, 47, 48, 49
Crow Indians, 109, 114
Culture, 61, 62
Curing songs, 20
Curly Headed Doctor, 64, 66, 67, 68, 69, 70, 72
  photograph, 71
Custer, George Armstrong, 107, 112

Dancing, 16, 58, 59, 62, 99
Death, beliefs about
  Apache, 39–40
  California Indians, 59
  potlatchers, 99

Pueblo, 25
Yuma, 59
Death masks, **94**
Deer Creek, 76, 77, 80
Democracy, 93
Dentalia, 90–92, 95
Desert People, 16
Digger Indians, 29
Disease, 24, 61, 74, 89, 98, 102
Divorce, 25, 59, 96
Dreamer Cult, 104–5, 108, 119
Dreams, 18
Drinking festival, 19
Dutch Reformed Church, 51
Duwamish Indians, 99

Eagle dance, 58
Earth, 105
Eastern Indians, 16
Elder Brother, 18

Feasts, 59
Filipinos, 97
Fire dance, 62
Fishing, 87, **91**
Fishing societies, 90, 92
Five Nations, 16
Florida, 50, 51
Food, 16, 24, 39, 57, 58, 59, 60, 87, 102
Fort Boise, 103
Fort Defiance, 31–32
Fort Fizzle, 111
Fort Hill, 103
Fort Leavenworth, 118
Fort Shaw, 112
Franciscan missionaries, 60–61
Fur trade, 97–98

Geronimo, Apache leader, 38, 40, 46–52
  death of, 51
  photograph, 50
  quoted, 48

Gibbon, Colonel, 112
    quoted, 113
Gift giving. See Potlatch
Gila River, 16
Gila Valley, 19
Gold rush, 61, 74, 98
Grand Ronde River, 107
Grant, Ulysses S., 72, 106–7
Great Painted Lady, 16, 19
Great Plains, 87
Green-Place-in-the-Rocks, 31

Hawaiians, 97
Hein-mot Too-ya-La-kekt (Chief Joseph), 121
Heliograph, 49
Hell's Canyon, 101
History, oral versus written records, 39–40
Hooker Jim, 64, 66, 70
    photograph, 71
Hopi (Hopitu) Indians, 16, 25, 29
Horses, 26, 37, 102
Hospitality, 57, 102
Houses, 92
Howard, General, 42, 43, 44, 107, 108, 109, 110, 111, 113, 117, 118, 119, 120
Hudson's Bay Company, 97–98
Hunting, 17, 25, 98, 102

Idaho, 84, 101, 107, 117, 119, 120
Indian Bureau, 34, 45–46, 48, 62, 64, 106
Indian scouts, 44–45, 47
Iroquois League, 16
Irrigation, 17, 19
Ishi, Yahi Indian, 73–82
    epitaph, 55
    photographs, 54, 78

Jack, Captain. See Captain Jack

Jeffords, Tom, 40, 42–43, 44
Jesuit missionaries, 20
Jesup, General, 116
Jewelry, 12, 58
Jim, Hooker. See Hooker Jim
Jimson weed, 59
Joseph the Elder, Nez Percé head man, 106
Joseph the Younger (Chief Joseph), Nez Percé leader, 104, 105, 107, 108, 111, 112, 114, 115, 116, 117
    death of, 120–21
    photograph, 84
    quoted, 117–18
    surrender of, 117, 119

Kachina dolls, 23
Kachinas, 23–24
Kansas, 118
Kearney, Stephen Watts, 30
King Georges, ships, 97
Kino, Father, 20
Kintpuash (Captain Jack), 64
Kiowa Apaches, 17
Kiowa Indians, 13, 16, 29
Klamath Indians, 64, 66
Klamath River, 111
Kroeber, Albert, 73–74, 79, 81, 82
Kwakiutl Indians, 89
    mask of, 94

Laguna Pueblo, 23
Land
    California Indians, 61–62
    Navajo, 33
    Nez Percé, 104, 105, 105–10
    Pima, 21
    Yana, 74
    See also Treaties
Land-of-Burnt-out-Fires, 64
Language, changes in, 39
Lapwai Reservation, 119

Lava beds, **65**
Lean Elk, Nez Percé leader, 114
Lewis and Clark expedition, 102, 105
Lolo Trail, 111
Long Walk (Navajo), 33, 51
Looking Glass the Elder, Nez Percé head man, 106
Looking Glass the Younger, Nez Percé leader, 107, 108, 109, 110, 112, 115
Lost brothers legends, 20, 26, 59–60
Lost River, 64
Louisiana Purchase, 102

Magnas Coloradas, Apache chief, 42, 46, 47
Maize, 17
Manuelito, Navajo chief, 34
Marriage, 25, 59, 88, 90
Masks, **94**
Massai, Apache warrior, 51
Medicine, 19
Medicine men
  Navajo, 28
  Pima and Papago, 19
  Pueblo, 24
  See also Kachinas; Shamans
Mescalero Apaches, 17, 51
Mexicans, 29, 30, 31, 40, 47, 48, 49, 50
Mexican War, 30
Mexico, 20, 27, 60
Miles, Nelson A., 49, 115, 116, 117, 118, 119
Military strategy, Apache, 39
Modoc War, 64–72, 107
Mohave Indians, 16
Montana, 114, 117, 118
Music, 62. See also Dancing; Singing
Mustaches, **91**

Names, 39, 80, 88, 92
Navajo Indians, 16, 21, 27–37
  destruction of, 33–34
  silverwork of, **35**
  uprising by, 32–33
Navajo Long Walk, 33, 51
New Mexico, 15, 16, 33
Nez Percé Indians, 84, 101–21
  Non-Treaty, 106, 107, 108, 110, 114, 117
  origin of name, 105
  Treaty, 105–6
Nimpau Indians, 105
Nobles, 93, 95, 98
Non-Treaty Nez Percé, 106, 107, 108, 110, 114, 117
Nootka Indians, 87, 88, 90, 98
North Dakota, 118, 120
Northern Indians, 16–17
Northwest Indians, 85–121

Oklahoma, 33, 51, 119, 120
Oregon, 64, 98, 101, 103, 104
Oregon Trail, 98, 103
Osceola Seminole chief, 116
Owls, 40

Pacific Northwest Indians, 85–121
Painting. See Rock Painting; Sand painting
Papago Indians, 16–22, 36
Peaceful People, 16, 22
Pima Indians, 16–22, 36
Plains Indians, 16
Platte River, 45
Poetry, 19, 26
Poker Joe, Nez Percé leader, 114, 115
Political units, 16
Pomo Indians, 62
Pontiac, Indian chief, 46

Pope, Dr., 79, 81, 82
  quoted, 82
Potlatch, 87, 88–101
Prayer sticks, 18
Presbyterian Mission, 119
Puberty rituals, 38, 59, 96
Pueblo Indians, 16, 22–27, 28,
  35, 99
Pueblo Revolt, 26, 28
Puritans, 90, 95

Quinault Indians, 89

Rabbitskin Leggings, Nez Percé
  leader, 103
Raiding, 17, 28, 29, 32, 37, 38
Rain, 17, 19–20, 22
Rain songs, 20, 23
Real People, 105
Red Beard (Tom Jeffords), 42
Religion
  Apache, 44
  California Indians, 57
  Navajo, 36
  potlatchers, 99
  Pueblo, 26
Reservations, 21, 27, 34, 40, 44,
  45–46, 64, 67, 72, 98, 107,
  109, 119
Rituals, 57
  puberty, 38, 59
  salmon, 88
River People, 16
Rock painting, 62–63
Roosevelt, Theodore, 51

Salmon, 87–88, 98, 102
  rituals, 88, **96**
Salmon River, 101
San Carlos Reservation, 47, 48,
  49, 50, 51
Sand painting, 25, 36–37
San Juan pueblo, 24

Santanta, Kiowa Indian, quoted,
  13
Sauk Indians, 121
Sculpture, wood, 92, **94**
Seattle, Chief, quoted, 99–101
Seminole Indians, 116
Seven Cities of Gold, 20
Shamans, 19, 62, 99
Sheep herding, 28
Sherman, William Tecumseh,
  113, 119
Shipping, 97
Shoshone Indians, 102
Silverwork, 35–36
Singing, 16, 19–20, 22–23, 58,
  62
Sioux Indians, 40, 107, 109, 116
Sitting Bull, 114, 115, 116, 117,
  118
Sky Father, 22
Slavery, 29–30, 38, 95
Small-group living, 16, 58
Smoke signals, 46
Snake River, 101, 107
Southwestern Indians, 16–52
Spain, 20, 27, 60
Spanish, 59
  Pima and Papago and, 20
  Pueblo and, 26–27
Spokane Indians, 104
Stronghold, Chiricahua Apaches,
  42–43
Stronghold, Modoc, 64, **65**
Sturgis, Major General, 114
Suquamish Indians, 99

Taboos, 39–40
Taos, Pueblo city, 16
Tattooing, 58
Taxation, 26
Tecumseh, Indian chief, 46
Thomas, Reverend, 67

Tlingit Indians, totem pole, **94**
Toohulhulsote, Nez Percé leader, 105, 107–8, 114, 115
Totem poles, 87, 92–93, **94,** 97
Trading, 29, 97–98, 102
Trail of Tears (Cherokee), 33, 50–51
Travois, **120**
Treaties
    California land, 61–62
    Nez Percé land, 105–6, 107, 108, 110, 114, 117
Treaty Nez Percé, 105–6

Umatilla Indians, unnamed chief of, quoted, 85
United States, 20, 21, 27, 30, 31, 40, 41, 49, 61
    Department of the Interior, 45
    Senate, 62, 106
    War Department, 45
    See also Indian Bureau; Reservations; Treaties
University of California, 73
Ute Indians, 29

Vancouver Island, 87, 89
Victorio, Apache head man, 45, 46
Visions, 58, 59, 93, 99

Wallowa Valley, 119
War making, 17, 25, 89, 95. *See also* Raiding
Washington, 89, 98, 99, 101, 103, 104

Waterman, Thomas, 79, 82
Wealth, 29, 39, 57, 89, 90–92, 93, 97
Weaving, 29, 35, 62
Wheat, 20
White Bird, Nez Percé leader, 112, 114, 115, 118
White Bird Canyon, 108, 109, 110
White Mountain Apaches, 17
White Painted Lady, 38
Whitman, Marcus, 103, 104
Wisconsin Sauk Indians, 121
Wiyot, Yuma god, 59
Women
    Apache, 38, 39
    California Indians, 58
    Navajo, 34–35
    Pima and Papago, 19
    Pomo, 62
    potlatchers, 96–97, 99
Wood, uses of, 92, **94**

Yahi Indians, **54,** 55, 73–82
Yana, Indian nation, 73–75
Yellowstone National Park, 113, 114
Yellowstone River, 114
Yellow Wolf, Nez Percé Indian, 104
Yuma Indians, 16, 59
Yurok Indians, 91, 95

Zuñi, Pueblo city, 16, 19